RELIGIOUS

FROM A 20th CENTURY ANALYTIC PHILOSOPHY PERSPECTIVE

Aamir Riyaz

CONTENTS

Page Nos.

CHAPTER-I
INTRODUCTION

My purpose in this thesis is to present an analysis of 'religious beliefs'. I have, in the main, compared and contrasted the notion of religious belief as found in Islamic philosophy and Wittgenstein's thought. Besides analysing the notion of religious beliefs as found in *The Quran,* I have in the main discussed the views of Mohammad Iqbal who is one of the leading exponents of Islamic thought.

Religious beliefs, according to Wittgenstein, do not purport to be statement of logical facts which can be true or false, they are the articulations of our faith. They are neither true nor false. One can even say that they are both true and false at the same time. The characterisation of truth and falsity does not apply to them. In his book, *On Certainty*[1] he says that the grounds of very few of our beliefs have ever been tested. Its grounds are not in themselves either true or false or grounded. He further says:

> "If the true is what is grounded, then the ground is not true, nor yet false."[2]

[1] L.Wittgenstein, *On Certainty,*ed. by G.E.M. Amscombe and G.H. von Wright, translated by Dennis Paul and G.E.M. Amscombe, NewYork and Evanston: J. & J. Harper Edition, 1968.

[2] *Ibid.,* 205, p. 33.

He further says that our religious beliefs are well-established, well-founded, and properly grounded and these are not only accidental features but an essential feature of them. Towards the end of his life he compared a religious believer with a tightrope walker. He says:

> "An honest religious thinker is like a tightrope walker. He almost looks as though he were walking on nothing, but air. His support is the slenderest imaginable. And yet it really is possible to walk on it."[3]

The foundational ground of religious beliefs in Islam is "Faith". The faith is in a form of life, in certain values, in certain practices, in the belief that these practices will lead to the realisation of the ends chosen by an individual. A man who sincerely adheres to *Iman* (faith), to Islam (complete submission to God) and is committed to *Ihsan* (doing good deeds) is a Muslim.

About religious beliefs, *The Quran*[4] *says*:

> "O ye who believe; believe in God and His apostle and the scriptures which He has sent to his apostle and the scriptures which he sent to those before. Anyone who denies God, His angels, His

3 L. Wittgenstein, *Culture and Value*, Basil Blackwell, Oxford, 1953, p. 73.

4 *The Holy Quran*, Text, Translation and Commentary by Abdullah Yusuf Ali, Kitab Bhavan, 2006.

> books, His apostle and the Day of Judgement has gone far, far astray." (4:136)

The word 'faith' is used in its wider sense in the authentic *Hadith* of the Prophet. It generally includes good deeds. Sometimes it simply is used as a synonym for the term 'good deeds'. Thus, the Prophet is reported to have said in one *Hadith*:

> "*Iman* (faith) has over sixty branches, and modesty (*haya*) is a branch of faith"[5]

In chapter two, I have discussed the nature of religious beliefs in *The Quran.* The issues which I have taken are: What is the ground of religious belief? Are religious beliefs grounded only in faith? The word 'faith' is used in two different senses in *The Quran.* According to Raghib, the famous lexicologist, faith is sometimes nothing more than a confession with tongue that one believes in *Allah* and Prophet. As has been said earlier the word faith is used in its wider sense in the authentic *Hadith* of the Prophet. It includes good deeds as well as a synonym for good deeds. A general misconception which prevails among Muslims as well as non-Muslims is that Islam does not give any importance to reason. *The Quran* exhorts us to make full use of our rational power. Some critics say that *The Quran* is not

---

[5] *Al-Bukhari*, Muhammad Muhsin Khan (Trans.), Kitab Bhavan, New Delhi, 1987, Vol. 1 Ch. 3, H.8.

grounded in any reasoning and based merely on faith. If Quranic teachings are beyond reasoning how can we understand them properly? In order to understand the teachings of *The Quran* we have to understand the five pillars on which Islam is founded. These are: (1) Believing in God, (2) Believing in His angels, (3) Believing in His messengers, (4) Believing in His books, (5) Believing in resurrection. I have also discussed the concept of *shirk* which is considered the gravest of all sins according to *The Quran. Allah* can forgive any kind of sin if He wishes but He will never forgive a person who does shirk. The opposite of Unity (*Tauhid*) is *shirk* (partner), implying partnership with *Allah. The Quran* considers *shirk* to be the most heinous crime. It says:

> "God forgives not that partners should be set up with Him; but He forgives anything else to whom He pleases; to set up partner with God is to devise a sin most heinous indeed." (4:48)

The Quran mentions the various forms of *shirk* which is summed up in the following verse:

> "Say: O people of the book, come to common terms as between us and you; that we worship none but *Allah* that we associate no partner with Him that we erect not from among ourselves Lords and patrons other than *Allah*." (3:64)

The most easily noticed form of *shirk* is that in which anything besides *Allah* is worshipped such as stones, idols, trees, animals, tombs, forces of nature or human beings who are supposed to be demi-gods or gods, or incarnation of God, or sons and daughters of God. The second kind of *shirk* which is less noticeable is the associating of other things with God which means that other things or beings possess the same form or attributes as possessed by Divine Being. The third kind of *shirk* is that in which some men take others as their Lords.

Of the different forms of *shirk*, idolatry is cited more frequently than all others and is denounced in *The Quran* in the most strong sense. During the advent of Islam it was most common throughout the world. Defending the idol worship some said that an idol is used only to enable a worshipper to concentrate his attention and become more deeply engrossed in Divine contemplation. To those who claim that a material symbols and idols help in one's concentration or meditation, *The Quran* answers in strong words that it is wrong to suppose that a material symbol is necessary for concentration, for attention can be every whit as easily concentrated on a spiritual object. It argues that only when the object of attention is spiritual that concentration helps the development of will power. *The Quran* also prohibits dedication to idols along with idol-worship.

In chapter three, I have discussed Iqbal's philosophy in general and the basis of his explanation of the tenets of Islam. After a discussion of his general philosophical approach, I have applied his method to the interpretation and analysis of religious beliefs. According to Iqbal, religion is not only a body of dogmas or rituals but a form of experience which ensures a grasp of nothing short of a direct and immediate illumination of the very core of reality also. Along with religious beliefs he also recognises the importance of other beliefs as the necessary pre-requisites for getting a comprehensive insight into the ultimate nature of the real, and towards spiritual upliftment of man. Iqbal, however, was not a philosopher in the sense of a system-builder like Plato. He never claimed to give a system of thought, although there is a complete system in his thought.

In chapter four, I have discussed the concept of religious belief and language-game as propounded by Later Wittgenstein. According to him, to grasp the meaning of a word we have to understand the role it plays in the language-game in which it is used. For Wittgenstein, religion is not a speculative affair but rather it is grounded in a kind of instinctual reaction. Through the notion of his analysis of the concept of language-game, he challenged the assertion that proofs or evidences have nothing to do with religious beliefs. The role of religion is important because it gives human being an avenue from which essential existential and religious question can be addressed. He vehemently said that reasons, evidences and proofs have nothing to do with the formulation of religious belief which is neither rational nor irrational but something separate and distinct from the concept of scientific rationality. There are varieties of rationality. The type of rationality that we use while seeing a film is different from the type of rationality that we use in our day to day life. Likewise, the rationality we employ while dealing with a child or an infant is radically different from the type of rationality we employ in dealing with the adults. So, it is wrong to think that the notion of rationality is one and the same in all spheres of activity. The rationality used in scientific enterprises cannot be regarded as 'the paradigm' of rationality. Though scientific rationality plays a role in science and scientific enterprises, it plays no role in the language-game of religion and other human activities.

In chapter five, I have discussed and contrasted Wittgenstein's and Islamic concept of religious beliefs. This chapter is divided into two sections. In section one; I have discussed the concept of religious beliefs according to Wittgenstein and Islam. In section two; I have discussed the points of similarities and differences between Islamic and Wittgenstein's concept of religious belief. According to Wittgenstein, religious belief is an absolute trust either in a book, in a being, in a holy man, in a prophet, in a doctrine, or all of them. Wittgenstein, by analysing the concept of religious belief says; "Believing means, submitting to an authority. Having once submitted to it, you cannot then, without rebelling against it, first call it in question and then once again find it convincing."[6] The same concept is repeated in *The Quran* (4:136), which I have quoted earlier in this chapter.

In chapter six, I have discussed Islam as a religion from scientific perspective. I have argued that, the misconception prevalent in the West namely that Islam is a non-progressive and static religion, and is antagonistic to science, progress and modern civilization, is totally baseless. I have shown the fact that it was only Islam which gave birth to modern science and started a scientific era in the world's history. It also can be regarded as the founder of modern civilization.

Concluding remarks form the seventh chapter of my thesis. In this chapter I have put forth in a summary form the findings of my thesis.

* * *

---

6 *Culture and Value,* op. cit., p. 52.

CHAPTER-II

NATURE OF RELIGIOUS BELIEFS (*IMAN*) IN *THE QURAN*

> Ghulami men na kam aati hain shamsheeren na tadbeeren
> Jo ho zauk-e-yakin paida to kat jati hain zanjeeren.
> (Neither thought nor swords works at the time of slavery
> It is only your staunch belief which cut the chain.)
>
> – Mohd. Iqbal, *Bal-e-Jibreel*

> I believe that one of the things Christianity says is that sound doctrines are all useless. That you have to change your life.
>
> – Ludwig Wittgenstein, *Culture and Value*

The word 'Belief' or 'Faith' is used in two different senses in *The Quran*. According to Raghib, the famous lexicologist, *Iman* is sometimes nothing more than a confession with the tongue that one believes in *Allah* and Prophet Mohammad. The following verse supports his contention:

> "Those who believe (in *The Quran*), and those who follow the Jewish scriptures and the Christians, and the sabians and anyone who believes in Allah and last day and work righteousness shall have their reward with their Lord: on them shall be no fear, nor shall they grieve." (2:62)

Again *Allah* says in *The Quran*:

> "O ye who believe; believe in God and His apostle, and the scripture which he has sent to his apostle and the scripture which He sent to those before (him). Anyone who denies God, His angels, His books, His apostle and the Day of Judgment, has gone far, far astray." (4:136)

Regarding the concept of 'Other', *The Quran* says:

> "Let there be no compulsion in religion: Truth stands out clear from error." (2:256)

This verse clearly says that compulsion is not compatible to the religion of Islam because; first, religion depends upon faith, trust and love, and these would be meaningless if imposed by some external force. Second, truth and error have been so clearly shown up by God that there should be no doubt in the minds of any person of good-will as to the fundamentals of faith. Third, God's protection is continuous and His plan is always to lead us from darkness to light.

It is further said in *The Quran:*

> "Say: O ye who reject faith; I worship not that which ye worship, nor will ye worship that which I worship and I will not worship that which ye worship, nor will ye worship that which I worship. To you is your religion and to me is mine." (109:1-6)

To maintain harmony among various religions *The Quran* gives solution and says:

> "Invite (all) to the way of thy Lord with wisdom and beautiful preaching; and argue with them in ways that are best and most gracious." (16:125)

The issues which come to my mind are: what is the ground of religious beliefs? Is religious belief grounded only in faith? Or it has some element of reason in itself. A general misconception which prevails among Muslims as well as non-Muslims is that Islam does not give any importance to reason. To remove this misconception in what follows I have discussed the five pillars of Islam. In other words, I have discussed the foundation on which the edifice of Islam is built.

The Quran exhorts us to make full use of our rational power. Some people say that the Holy scriptures are beyond reasoning. If they are beyond reasoning then the question arises how can we understand them properly or authentically? Man has been granted a mind which enables him to think, and through the instrumentality of intellect in building a system of knowledge. Reason converts the raw material collected by the senses into knowledge. *The Quran* rightly assigns to 'reason' and 'intellect' an important role in human life:

> "The worst of beasts in Allah's sight are the deaf, the dumb, who do not use their intellect to understand." (8:22)

This verse of *The Quran* degrades the status of the man when he does not press reason to his service. *The Quran* says that such a man not only lives a worthless and debased life in this world but is not fit to live in the higher plane on which he enters after death. *The Quran* further says:

> "They have hearts with which they discern not and they have eyes with which they see not, and they have ears with which they hear not; these are as the cattle; nay are worse; they are the heedless." (7:179)

In *The Quran*, human reason is repeatedly praised. It is clearly stated that even divine revelation is not to be accepted unquestioningly and uncritically. Man is persuaded to think over it and interpret it in the light of his reason. It is said in *The Quran*:

> "Do they not consider *The Quran* with care? Had it been from other than God, they would surely have found therein much discrepancy." (4:82)

The Quran insists that even success in war depends on the right use of reason. It is generally believed that an army which is inspired with courage and fired with zeal is sure to win. The *'Nabi'* is enjoined not to demand blind obedience from men but to exhort them to think and ponder. The following verse leaves no scope for doubt that *The Quran* encourages independent thinking:

> "Say; I exhort you into one thing. And what is that one thing? It is that ye awake, for *Allah's* sake by two's and singly. And then reflect." (34:46)

The Quran expects man to think and use his power of understanding. If he does this he will be sure to follow the right path. The point to bear in mind is that the path which leads to success, that is eligibility for a higher plane of existence, can be discovered and followed only with the combined help of reason and revelation. These sources of guidance are supplementing each other. If they are kept within their proper sphere, there will be no conflict between them. *The Quran* lays stress on the value of correct knowledge and advises us to accept it and act upon it. All else is dismissed as mere guess work which is far from being a trustworthy guide to action. As *Allah* says in *The Quran*:

> "A guess can never take the place of truth." (53:28)

From this it follows that as rational beings, it is our duty not to stop till we have achieved correct knowledge. To be content with a mere guess is to denounce our rationality.

The Quran gives a sketch of the process of knowing which is both scientific and ethical. The process is begun by the activity of senses which furnishes the raw material of knowledge. The next stage is that of attending when the mind addresses itself to the material reaching it. This is the stage of perceptual knowledge. The sense data are referred to external objects and events and their objective meaning is grasped. In the third stage, through the process of analysis, synthesis, abstraction and generalization the material is converted into knowledge of varying degree of generality. The final stage is that of comprehension in which the new knowledge is placed and viewed in the context of the totality of human knowledge and experience. At this stage knowledge and its meaning for human life is assessed. *The Quran* exhorts men to aim at this deeper understanding of the meaning of *Nabi's* words, whenever he speaks to them. It denounces those who fail to make this attempt and stop at the first or second stage, being content with imperfect knowledge.

What *The Quran* is driving at is that a man, whose mind is clouded with prejudices and preconceptions, will not be able to apprehend the truth. To apprehend it, he must approach it with an open and unbiased mind, must concentrate his attention upon it and must strive to comprehend it in relation to his genuine knowledge and authentic experience. In effect, *The Quran* recommends them an *'a posteriori'* approach to revelation. By implication, *The Quran* does not favour *'a priori'* approach.

Even many Muslims feel that one should avoid getting into a debate on religious issues. But this is not so. *Allah* encourages reasoning and discussion in *The Quran* in the following verse:

> "Invite all to the way of thy lord with wisdom and beautiful preaching and argue with them and reason with them in the ways that are best and most gracious." (16:125)

In *The Quran* the Arabic word '*Qalu*' which means 'they say' is mentioned 332 times; and the Arabic word '*Qul*' which means 'say' is also mentioned 332 times. This proves that *The Quran* encourages discussion. There is no conflict between revelation and reason, rather they supplement each other. *Iman* both in revelation and reason together enrich life and make it fruitful, provided each keeps to its own proper sphere. Faith energizes reason and reason orientates faith to concrete reality. Reason without faith is like a well-constructed machine which is not attached to a motor while faith without reason is only a blind force. The glorious periods in human history were characterized by a robust faith and an active reason. Prof. Whitehead has rightly remarked:

"Ages of faith are the ages of rationalism."[1]

Regarding the ground of religious belief it is said that it is dependent on faith which in turn has six pillars which I have discussed later in this chapter in detail.

The word 'faith' is used in its wider sense in the authentic *Hadiths* of the Prophet, that is to say, as including good deeds and sometimes simply as standing for good deeds. Thus, the Prophet is reported to have said in one *Hadith*:

> "*Iman* (faith) has over sixty branches, and modesty (*haya*) is a branch of faith."[2]

Allah says in *The Quran*:

> "It is not righteousness that you turn your faces to the East and the West (in prayer); but righteousness is he who believes in *Allah* and the last day and the angels and the Book (Holy Scripture) and the Prophets." (2:177)

It is again stated by Sahih Muslim in his *Book of Iman* (faith):

---

1 M. Iqbal, *The Reconstruction of Religious Thought in Islam*, Lahore, 1930, p. 2.

2 *Al-Bukhari,* op. cit.,Vol. 1, Book 2; Ch.3; H.8.

"A person approaches Prophet and asks what faith is? He replies that faith is believe in *Allah*, in his angels, his books, his meetings, his messengers, in the resurrection and in the destiny."[3]

So basically there are six pillars of faith in Islam:

(1) Believing in God,

(2) Believing in his angels,

(3) Believing in his messengers,

(4) Believing in his books,

(5) Believing in predestination,

(6) Believing in resurrection.

Now I will discuss each one separately:

(1) Believing in God:

The concept of God is taken as axiomatic truth in almost all religions and in all religious books. To prove the existence of a Supreme Being *The Quran* advances numerous arguments about who are the creators and controllers of this universe. These arguments are of three kinds. The first argument is drawn from the creation, which relate to the material or lower experience of humanity. The second argument is based

---

[3] *Sahih Muslim,* Abdul Hamid Siddiqi (trans.), Kitab Bhavan, New Delhi, 2000, Vol. 1; Ch.2; H.6.

on the evidence of human nature, which concerns the inner experience of humanity. The third category of argument is based on divine revelation to man which may be called the higher or spiritual experience of humanity.

The first argument drawn from the creation, centers round the word *'Rabb'*. In the very first revelation that came to the Prophet, he was told by *Allah*, in *The Quran*:

"Read in the name of *'Rabb'* who created?" (96:1)

The word *'Rabb',* which is generally translated as 'Lord', carries a different significance. According to the best authorities on Arabic lexicology, it combines two senses, that of fostering, bringing up or nourishing and that of regulating, completing and accomplishing. According to Raghib, *'Rabb'* signifies the fostering of a thing in such a manner as to make it attain one condition after another until it reaches its goal of perfection.

The second kind of argument for the existence of God relates to the human soul. There is an inner light within each man which tells him that there is a higher being, a god, a creator. Sometimes this consciousness on the part of the human soul is mentioned in terms of its unimaginable nearness to the Divine spirit. It is said in *The Quran:*

"We are nearer to him than his life-vein." (50:16)

And again,

"We are nearer to it (the soul) than you." (56:86)

The idea that God is near to man than even his own self or soul only shows that the awareness of the existence of God in the human soul is part of its very existence. God and soul are one. Just as the existence of soul cannot be questioned, likewise the existence of God cannot be questioned. Both are self-evident. Their truth is derived from the respective concepts themselves.

The third argument relates to the Divine revelation, the clearest and surest evidence, which not only establishes the truth of the existence of God but also throws light on the Divine attributes without which the existence of the Divine Being would remain a mere dogma. It is through this disclosure of the Divine attributes that belief in God becomes the most important factor in the evolution of man. God nourishes everything in the universe, He is loving and affectionate to His creatures, so one who believes in Him will be moved by the impulse of love and affection towards His creator. God is merciful and forgiving. From these attributes of God it follows that His servants must be merciful and forgiving to their fellow-beings.

Islam accepts the Unity of God, which is expressed in *The Quran* in the form of '*laillaha ill-Allah*'. It is made up of four words, *la* (no), *ilaha* (that which is expressed), *illa* (except) and *Allah* (the popular name of the Divine Being). Thus these words, which are commonly rendered into English as meaning 'there is no god but *Allah*', convey the significance that there is nothing which deserves to be worshipped except *Allah.* When this confession is combined with the confession of the prophethood of Muhammad, *'Muhammad-ur-Rasulu-llah'* then it admits a man into the fold of Islam. The Unity of God implies that God is one in His person, one in His attributes and one in His work. His oneness in His person means that there is neither plurality of gods nor plurality of persons in the Godhead. His oneness in attributes implies that no other being possesses one or more of the Divine attributes in perfection.

The best definition of God and the doctrine of unity are beautifully summed up in one of the shortest chapter of *The Quran* i.e. *"Sura Ikhlas"* (purity of faith). It goes as follows:

> "Say: He is God, the one and only; He is the eternal, the absolute; He begets not nor He is begotten; and there is none like unto Him." (112:1-4)

To explain this *'Sura'*, the first thing we have to note is that His nature is so sublime, so far beyond our limited conception that the best way in which we can realize Him is to feel that He is a real concrete existence, not a mere abstraction of thought. He is near us; He cares for us; we owe our existence to Him. Secondly, He is the one and only God, only one to whom worship is due and all other things or beings that we can think of are His creatures and in no way comparable to Him. Thirdly, He is eternal, without beginning or end, absolute, not limited by time or place or circumstances. He is the reality before which all other things or places are mere shadow or reflection. Fourthly, we must not think of Him as having a son or a father for that would be to import human qualities into our conception of Him. Fifthly, He is not like any other person or things that we know or can imagine. His qualities and nature are unique.[4]

The idea of God in *The Quran* is different from the idea of Polytheism, a system in which people believe in many gods and many Lords. Polytheism, according to Quranic interpretation is opposed to deeper understanding of life. If life has a unity in its design then the unity in design, unity in the fundamental facts of existence, proclaim the unity of maker.

---

4 *The Holy Quran,* op. cit., p. 1806, ref. no. 6296.

The opposite of Unity (*Tauhid*) is *shirk* (partner), implying partnership. In *The Quran*, *shirk* is used to signify the association of gods with God. In *The Quran shirk* is supposed to be the gravest of all sins. About *shirk, The Quran* comments categorically that:

> "Surely, ascribing partner to Him (shirk) is a grievous iniquity." (31:13)

Again, *The Quran* considers *shirk* to be the most heinous crime. It says:

> "God forgives not that partners should be set up with Him; but He forgives anything else to whom He pleases; to set up partner with God is to devise a sin most heinous indeed." (4:48)

The Quran mentions the various forms of *shirk* which is summed up in the following:

> "Say: O people of the book, come to common terms as between us and you; that we worship none but *Allah* that we associate no partner with Him that we erect not from among ourselves Lords and patrons other than *Allah*." (3:64)

The most easily noticed form of *shirk* is that in which anything besides *Allah* is worshipped such as stones, idols, trees, animals, tombs, forces of nature or human beings who are supposed to be demi-gods or gods, or incarnation of God, or sons and daughters of God. The second kind of *shirk* which is less noticeable is the association of other things with God which means that other things or beings possess the same form or attributes as possessed by Divine Being. The third kind of *shirk* is that in which some men take others as their Lords. The Prophet himself explained this by answering a question which was posed to him. In one verse of *The Quran, Allah* says:

> "They (Jews and Christians) have taken their doctors of law and their monks for Lords besides *Allah.*" (9: 31)

A convert Muslim, said to the Prophet that the Jews and the Christians did not worship the doctors of law and the monks. The Prophet asked him if it was not true that they blindly obeyed them in what they enjoined and what they forbade, and he answered in affirmation. This report shows that to follow the order of great men blindly was also considered *shirk.* The fourth kind of *shirk* is referred to in this verse:

> "Hast thou seen him who takes his low desires for his god?" (25:43)

Here the blind submission to one's own desire is described as a form of *shirk.* Thus, belief in the Unity of God means that true obedience is due to God alone and to no one else. Whosoever obeys either anyone else or his own low desires in preference to the Divine commandments, is really guilty of *shirk.*

Of the different forms of *shirk*, idolatry is cited more frequently than all others and is denounced in *The Quran* in the most strong sense. During the advent of Islam it was most common throughout the world. Defending the idol worship some said that an idol is used only to enable a worshipper to concentrate his attention and become more deeply engrossed in Divine contemplation. To those who claim that a material symbols and idols help in one's concentration or meditation, *The Quran* answer in strong words that it is wrong to suppose that a material symbol is necessary for concentration, for attention can be every whit as easily concentrated on a spiritual object. It argues that only when the object of attention is spiritual that concentration helps the development of will power. *The Quran* also prohibits dedication to idols along with idol-worship.

(2) Belief in Angels:

The word used, in *The Quran* for angel is *'Malak'*, the plural of which is *'Malaika'*. *The Quran* does not speak of the origin of angels but it does speak about the origin of the several *jinns*. *The Quran* speaks of the creation of man from dust and of *jinns* from fire. However, there is a report from Hazrat Aisha, according to which the Prophet said that the *jinns* are created from fire and that the angels are created from light (*Nur*).[5] This

[5] *Sahih Muslim*, op. cit., 53:10.

Hadith of Prophet shows that the angels are immaterial beings and *jinns* and angels are two different classes of beings and to consider them as belonging to one class is a mistake.

Allah says in *The Quran:*

> "Praise is to *Allah*, who created the heaven and earth out of nothing who made the angels messengers with wings." (35:1)

It is commonly thought that the immaterial beings (angels) can assume any shape but this idea is not supported by *The Quran*. It is mentioned in *The Quran* that the angels, who were sent to help the believers were not seen by the human eye.

Allah says in *The Quran*:

> "But *Allah* did pour His calm on the Apostle and on the believers and sent down forces which you do not see." (9:26)

The Quran further states that the devils or *jinns* cannot be seen by the human eye. *The Quran* mentions this in the following verse:

> "O ye children of Adam; let not Satan seduce you in the manner as he got your parents out of the garden, stripping them of their raiment, to expose their shame because he and his tribe watch you from a position where you cannot see them. We made the evil ones friends to those without faith." (7:27)

Though angels are spoken of as beings, they are not given with power of discrimination like human beings. Their function is to obey *Allah* and they cannot disobey. It is mentioned in *The Quran:*

> "They do not disobey *Allah* in that which He commands them but do as they are commanded." (66:6)

It is commonly accepted in Islam that angel Gabriel came to the Prophet with the Divine revelation. The Prophet received Gabriel and his messages with the spiritual senses. He did not see Gabriel with the physical eyes. In some incidents he received the revelation while he was sitting with his companions yet no one of them ever saw the angle or even heard his voice.

The most prominent function of the angel is the bringing down of Divine revelation or the communication of Divine message to the prophets. The angel, for the prophets, is a reality because the prophets not only see the angel but also hear his voice. As the angels are immaterial beings the Prophet sees Gabriel sometimes in the shape of a human being and sometimes in other forms. According to *The Quran*, the angel who brought revelation to the Prophet is known by the name of Gabriel. The Arabic form of Gabriel is '*Jibrail*' which means the 'servant of God'. Gabriel is also mentioned in *The Quran* as '*Ruh al-Amin*' or the "Faithful Spirit" (26:193-

194), and '*Ruh-al-Qudus'* or the "Holy Spirit" (16:102). In all these places, *Gabriel* or the Faithful Spirit or the Holy Spirit is said to have revealed *The Quran* to the Prophet.

In one *Hadith* Gabriel is spoken of as the great angel who is entrusted with secret message and in *The Quran* (42:51), Gabriel is called the messenger through whom God speaks to His Prophets.

The second function of the angels is to strengthen the righteous servants of God and to give them comfort in trial and suffering. Regarding this Jesus Christ is especially mentioned because of the allegation of the Jews against him. In *The Quran* it is mentioned thrice that Jesus Christ was endowed with the Holy Spirit, which is another name for *Gabriel.* This endowment gave him his strength. Firstly it is mentioned in *The Quran*:

> "We gave 'Moses' the book and followed him up with a succession of Apostle and we gave Jesus the son of 'Mary' clear signs and strengthened him with the Holy Spirit." (2: 87)

That Jesus Christ was strengthened with the Holy spirit is also mentioned in *The Quran* in chapter 2, verse no. 253 and chapter 5, verse no. 110.

Another important function of the angels is that of intercession which includes both the believers and the unbelievers. Intercession is really a prayer to God on behalf of the sinners on the Day of Judgment but it is said that angels pray for men even in this life. It is said in *The Quran*:

> "The angels celebrate the praise of their Lord and ask forgiveness for those on earth." (42:5)

As a result of the prayers of the angels, the faithful are actually guided forth from every kind of darkness into light.

It will be seen that in his spiritual function the angel is meant to render help in the spiritual advancement of man. The angel brings Divine revelations and it is only with the help of such revelations that man is able to realize what the spiritual life is and to make advancement spiritually through the development of his inner faculties. The angel's intercession and prayer even for the unbeliever are undoubtedly meant to set him on the road to spiritual progress. The angels bringing of the believers from darkness into light and his blessing on the Prophet are the advancement of the cause of spiritual progress of the concerned persons. Now, therefore, if we analyze each one of the functions of the angel we find that it is aimed at helping the spiritual advancement of man and lead him to spiritual perfection.

Another function of the angels, on which special stress is laid in *The Quran*, is to keep a record of the good and evil deeds of man. These angels are called "honorable recorder" (*Kiram-an-Katibin*). The word is mentioned in the following verses of *The Quran*:

> "And surely there are keepers over you, honorable recorders, they know what you do." (82:10-12)

Again the angels called *Kiram-an-katibin* are mentioned in *The Quran*:

> "When the two receivers receive, sitting on the right and on the left, he utters not a word but there is by him a watcher at hand." (50:17-18)

The different functions of angel in the spiritual world are thus connected either with the awakening of the spiritual life in man or its advancement and progress. *The Quran* gives reasons why faith in angels is required along with a faith in God:

> "Righteous is the one who believes in *Allah* and the last day and the angels, and the Book and the Prophet." (2:177)

The Quran again says:

"The messenger believes in what has been revealed to him from his Lord and so do the believers. They all believe in *Allah* and His angels and His books and His messengers." (2:285)

Faith in angels, therefore, means that there is a spiritual life for man and that he must develop that life by working in accordance with the prompting of the angel and by bringing into play the faculties which God has given him. That is why *The Quran* requires a belief in angels and a disbelief in devils. This does not mean that one must deny the existence of the devils. This only means that one must obey the commandments of God and refuse to follow the suggestions of the devil. Faith in the angels, therefore, only means that every good suggestion, which is the suggestion of the angel, must be accepted because it leads to the spiritual development of man.

(3) Belief in His Messengers:

The next article of faith in Islam is belief in the Prophets. The Arabic word for Prophet is *'Nabi'*. Some lexicologist explains the word '*Nabi*' as meaning an ambassador between God and rational beings from among his creatures. According to some other, a '*Nabi*' is the man who gives information about God. A '*Nabi*' is also called a '*rasul*' which means an apostle or messenger. The word '*Nabi*' and '*rasul*' are used interchangeably in *The Quran* because of the two capacities which a Prophet has. These capacities are the capacity to receive information from God and the capacity to impart that information to mankind. In his first capacity he is called a '*Nabi*' and in the second one, a '*rasul*'.

Islam accepts faith in Divine revelation as essential. Since revelation is communicated through a man, therefore faith in the messenger is naturally implied.

The prophets are not only the bearer of the Divine message but he also shows how that message is to be interpreted in practical life and therefore he is the model, the paradigm to be followed. It is the Prophet's example that inspires a living faith in the hearts of his followers and brings about a real transformation in their lives. That is why *The Quran* lays special stress on the fact that the Prophet must be a human being.

As *Allah* says in *The Quran*:

> "Before thee, also, the apostles we sent were but men to whom we granted inspiration. If you do not realize this, ask to those who possess message." (21:7)

The message is further revealed in *The Quran* when *Allah* says:

> "We did not give them bodies that ate no food and they are not exempt from death." (21:8)

These two verses clarify that the messengers are just a man like us. This is true because the entire apostle sent by God were men not angels or another kind of beings who could not understand men or whom men could not understand. As men they were subject to all the laws governing the physical bodies of men. They ate and drank and their bodies perished in death.

The difference between the messengers and angels lies in the fact that messengers like other human beings are material beings and are chosen from them to deliver the messages of *Allah* to other human beings. Angels on the other hand are different creation altogether. They are not like human beings and are immaterial beings. They may come on the earth in any form or shape like animals, birds or in any other symbolic form. Angels, unlike messengers, are not created out of fine clay but they are created out of *Nur* (light) of *Allah.* In *The Quran,* more than one lakh messengers are mentioned out of which only twenty five are mentioned by their names. The numbers of angels is not specified in *The Quran* but their population is said to be more than that of human beings. The function of angels is to obey the commandments of *Allah.* They are created in such a way that they cannot disobey *Allah* by their free-will. Messengers received the revelations of *Allah* only through the angels and delivered it to the mankind. Angels, unlike messengers, are immaterial beings. We can see messengers with the human eye but we cannot see angels. Not even messengers could see angels with the human eye.

The Quran, however, not only establishes the theory that Prophets have appeared in all nations but it goes further and says that it is necessary that a Muslim should believe in all those Prophets. According to *The Quran*, there is no nation in the world in which a Prophet has not appeared. *The Quran* says:

> "For every nation there is a messenger." (10:47)

Every generation or nation has its message or messenger. God revealed himself to it in some way or another. If those messengers were ignored or rejected or their messages were twisted or misused, the Day of Judgment will come when perfect justice will be done and the whole truth will be revealed. We are further told that there have been Prophets besides those mentioned in *The Quran*:

> "And we sent messengers we have mentioned to thee before and messengers we have not mentioned to thee." (4:164)

It is stated in a *Hadith* that there have been 1, 24,000 prophets on the face of the earth, while *The Quran* contains only about twenty-five names.

In fact to believe in some prophets and reject others is condemned as unbelief *(Kufr)*. *The Quran* clearly speaks about it:

> "Those who disbelieve in *Allah* and His Messengers and desire to make a distinction between *Allah* and these Messengers and say we believe in some and disbelieve in others and desire to take a course in between these are truly disbelievers." (4:150-151)

A belief in all the Prophets of the world is thus an essential principle of Islam and though the faith of Islam is summed up in two sentences. There are first, that "there is no god but *Allah* and Muhammad is His apostle." It means anyone who confesses belief in Muhammad accepts all the prophets of the world whether their names are mentioned in *The Quran* or not. Prophets appeared in every nation but their message was limited to that particular nation and in some cases to one or a few generation but these prophets were national (local) prophets. The final step, therefore, in the institution of prophethood was the coming of one prophet for the entire humanity. The day world-prophet, Prophet Mohammad, attained prophecy all other (local) prophets became irrelevant. The national prophets are illustrated by *The Quran*:

> "We sent 'Moses' with our signs and command to bring out thy people from the depths of darkness into light." (14:5)

The Quran further speaks of Jesus as a messenger to the children of Israel and *Allah* says:

> "And appoint him as a messenger to the children of Israel." (3:49)

Regarding Prophet Muhammad *The Quran* unequivocally says:

> "Say, O mankind, surely I am the messenger of *Allah* to you all; of Him whose is the kingdom of the heavens and the earth." (7:158)

One thing is sure that no other Prophet is spoken of either in *The Quran* or in any of the *Hadith* as having been sent to the whole of humanity or to all people or all nations; nor is Prophet Muhammad ever spoken of in *The Quran* as having been sent to his people only. Prophet Muhammad is spoken of as the last of the Prophets in *The Quran*. As *The Quran* says:

> "Muhammad is not the father of any of your men but he is the messenger of Allah and the last of the prophets and *Allah* is ever knower of all things." (33:40)

(4) Belief in His Books:

The Quran and the authentic *Hadiths* are the most authentic sources of Islam. For every Muslims to believe in *The Quran* and the *Hadith* is an article of faith. The original source from which all principles and ordinances of Islam are drawn is the holy book called *Al-Quran*. Generally the sources are said to be four. Its sources are the following:

(a) *The Quran*;

(b) The *sunna* or *Hadith*; i.e. doing and sayings of the Prophet Muhammad;

(c) *Ijma* or unanimous agreement of the Muslim community; and

(d) *Qiyas* or Reasoning.

The first two are called absolutely sure arguments and the latter two are called argument obtained by exertion. *'Ijma'* and *'Qiyas'* are based on *The Quran* and *Hadith. The Quran* is actually the real foundation on which the whole super-structure of Islam rests. It is perfectly right to say that *The Quran* is the sole source from which all the teachings and practices of Islam are drawn. It was revealed in the month of '*Ramadhan*' on a certain night which is known as the 'Night of Majesty'. *Allah* himself mentions it in *The Quran*:

> "'Ramadhan' is the month in which *The Quran* was sent down as a guide to mankind and also clears signs for guidance and judgment." (2:185)

The Quran was revealed in parts and each of the parts was written and communicated to memory as soon as it was revealed and the total revelation took more than twenty two years of the Prophet's life. Though it was revealed in parts through Gabriel yet the entire revelation is one whole, delivered in identical manner. The revelation generally comes in three forms:

The first mode is called '*wahy*' (revelation).The inspired word, which enters the hearts of the Prophets and of the righteous is called '*wahy*' because it is like a sudden suggestion made directly to the heart of the inspired one. It is not a message in words but simply an idea which comes like a flash and clears up a doubt or difficulty and it is not the result of meditation. The second mode is described as speaking from behind a veil carrying a deeper significance, is shown as in a vision or in a dream. The third mode is that in which the angel bearing the message is delivered in words. This is the highest form of revelation. While the first two lower forms of revelation are common to Prophets as well as those who are not Prophets, the third mode of revelation is limited to the Prophets of God only.

The Prophet from time to time had seen visions but his first experience of higher revelation was when he was alone in the cave of *'Hira'*. It is clearly mentioned in one of the *Hadith* of the Prophet Muhammad:

> "He (Gabriel) squeezed me and squeezed me to such an extent that I was quite exhausted and this was repeated thrice."[6]

The second message came to him after an interval of some months and the effect was so great that on the coldest of days perspiration would run down his forehead. In one of the *Hadith,* Aisha, his wife says:

> "I saw revelation coming down upon him in the severest cold and when that condition was over perspiration ran down his forehead."[7]

Though *The Quran* was revealed in parts, yet it is a mistake to suppose that it remained long in those fragmentary conditions. *The Quran* is itself clear on this point and says:

> "And those who reject faith say: Why is not *The Quran* been revealed to him all at once? Thus (it is revealed) that we may strengthen thy heart thereby, and we have rehearsed it to thee in slow, well-arranged stages, gradually." (25:32)

Thus, the arrangement of *The Quran* was a part of Divine scheme. Another verse showing that the collection of the Book was a part of the Divine scheme runs thus:

---

6 *Sahih Al-Bukhari*, op. cit., 1:1.
7 *Ibid.*, 1:1.

"Surely on us rests the collecting of it and the reciting of it."[8]

It appears from this that just as *The Quran* was recited by Gabriel to the Prophet, in like manner; the collecting of its various parts was effected by the Prophet under the guidance of the Holy Spirit.

A European writer gives his opinion about *The Quran* in his well-known book, *'Preliminary Discourse'* and says:

> "The style of *The Quran* is generally beautiful and fluent... and in many places especially where the majesty and attributes of God are described, sublime and magnificent. He succeeded so well and so strangely captivated the minds of his audience that several of his opponents thought it the effect of witchcraft and enchantment."[9]

Sunnah or Hadith (the saying and Tradition of Prophet Muhammad) is the second and undoubtedly, secondary source from which the teachings of Islam are drawn. There are three kinds of *Sunnah.* Firstly, it may be a saying of the Prophet which has a bearing on a religious question, secondly an action or a practice of his and thirdly his silent approval of the action or practice of another. During the Prophet's life time it became necessary to transfer the

---

[8] *Ibid.*, 75:17.

[9] *A Comprehensive Commentary On The Quran,* Translation and preliminary discourse by Sale, G., Boston: Houghton, University of Toronto, 1927, p. 48

messages from one person to another taught by him. In fact the Prophet himself gave instruction for it in one *Hadith:*

> "Go back to your people and teach them these things."[10]

There is evidence that on one occasion the Prophet, while teaching Muslims the duty of holding sacred each other's life, property, and honour said:

> "He who is present here should carry this message to him who is absent."[11]

The collection of Tradition was in stages. At the first stage the preservation of Traditions were taken in the lifetime of the Prophet. The names of Abu Hurairah and Aisha (Prophets' wife) are very important regarding this. Abu Hurairah, who would remain in the Prophet's company at all cost and store up in his memory everything which the Prophet said or did. Hazrat Aisha was also one of those who sought to preserve the practice of the Prophet. She had a marvellous memory and was gifted with a clear intellect by virtue of which she refused to accept anything which she did not understand. It is said:

---

10 *Sahih Al-Bukhari*, op.cit., 3:25.

11 *Ibid.*, 3:37.

"She never heard anything she did not recognize but she questioned about it again and again."[12]

The collection of Tradition entered at the second stage with the Prophet's death. Every case, that came up for decision is to be referred either to *The Quran* or to some judgment or saying of the Prophet and therefore obtained a wide reputation. The other factor which was of utmost importance gave impetus to the knowledge of Tradition at this stage that to the companions of the Prophet, the religion which he had brought was so priceless that they valued it above all else in the world.

At the third stage, there were no more reports to be investigated from different persons and now the whole Tradition was the property of teachers who taught at various centres and, therefore, in the third stage, it could all be learnt by visiting these centres, instead of enquiring about it from individuals. At this stage, moreover, the writing of Tradition became more common.

Before the middle of the second century, at the fourth stage, Tradition started to assume a more permanent shape and written collections began to see the light of the day. Hundreds of the students were engaged in the work of learning Tradition at various centres but with every new teacher and

12 *Ibid.*, 3:35.

student the work of preserving the name of the transmitter along the text was becoming more difficult.

In the third century of *Hijrah,* this great work was brought to completion. This time two kinds of collections were made, *Musnad* and *Jami* or *Musannaf.* The *Musnad* (earlier type) were arranged not according to the subject-matter of the Tradition but under the name of the companion on whose final authority the report rested. It was because of the second one i.e. *Musannaf* (later type) that the Tradition came to perfection. The *Jami* arranges reports according to their subject-matter. Under this six books are recognised as *Bukhari, Muslim, Abu Dawud, Tirmidzi, Ibn Majah* and *Nasai*. These books classified reports under various subjects and thus made the Tradition easy for references, not only for lawyers and judges but also for students and research scholars thus giving a further impetus to the study of the Tradition.

(5) Belief in Predestination:

The Arabic word for predestination is *Qadar* which means the making manifest of the measure of a thing or simply measure. It is the law or the ordinance or the measure which is working throughout the creation. In the language of *The Quran,* it is the universal law of God which is applicable to men as well as to the nature extending to the sun, the moon, the stars, the earth and the heavens and all that exist in them. As *Allah* says in *The Quran*:

> "Glorify the name of thy Lord, the most High, who hath created and further, given order and proportion, who hath ordained laws and granted guidance." (87:1-3)

It is further said in *The Quran:*

> "It is He to whom belongs the domain of the heavens and the earth. He has no begotten son, nor has He a partner in His dominion. It is He who created all things and ordered them in due proportion." (25:2)

(6) Faith in Life after Death:

A faith in life after death is the last of the basic principle of Islam. According to *The Quran*, death is not the end of a man's life. It only opens the door to another, a higher form of life. As *Allah* says in *The Quran:*

> "We have decreed death to be your common lot, and we are not to be frustrated and from changing your forms and creating you (again) in (forms) that ye know not." (56:60-61)

Just as from the small life-germ grows the man and he does not lose his individuality for all the changes which he undergoes, so from this man is made the higher man. That this new life is a higher form of life is also discussed in *The Quran:*

> "See how we have bestowed more on some than on others. But verily the hereafter is more in rank and gradation and more in excellence." (17:21)

It means individuals should not suppose that all gifts are of equal value. The spiritual one ranks far higher in dignity and real worth than the transitory one. Therefore, it is altogether worth to compare the worldly prosperity of a wicked man with the apparent want of it to a man of spiritual worth. There is no comparison between them when measured by right standard.[13]

The Quran not only speaks of a life after death which opens out for man a new world of advancement before which the progress of this life sinks into insignificance. It also shows that the basis of that life is laid in this life. The hereafter is not a mystery beyond the grave. It begins in this life. For the good, the heavenly life and for the wicked, a life in hell begins even here though the limitations of this life do not allow most people to realize this. As *Allah* says in *The Quran*:

---

[13] *The Holy Quran*, op. cit., Ref. 2201, p. 700.

"Thou wast indeed heedless of this, but now we have removed from thee thy veil, so thy sight is sharp this day." (50:22)

This shows that the spiritual life which is hidden from the human eye by reason of material limitation, will become manifest in the resurrection because human perception will then be clear, the veil of material limitation having been removed.

The whole of creation on this earth is for the service of man and human life has some aim and purpose to fulfill is one of the arguments for resurrection advanced by *The Quran*.

As *Allah* says in *The Quran*:

"Does man think that he will be left uncontrolled or without any purpose (him)." (75:36)

It has many implications: (1) uncontrolled, free to do what he likes; (2) without any moral responsibility, not accountable for his action; (3) without a purpose, useless; (4) forsaken.

Allah again says in *The Quran*:

"Do you then think that we have created you in vain and that you will not be returned to us?" (23:115)

Just as the God-idea ennobles man's life and endows it with the purest and highest impulses so does the resurrection-idea introduce seriousness into man's life which otherwise cannot be attained. God's creation is not without a higher serious purpose. It is not vain or for mere play or sport. If everything in nature is intended for the service of man, human life itself could not be without purpose. *The Quran* refers to this argument in the following verse:

> "Certainly we have created man in the best then we render him the lowest of the low except those who believe and do good, so their's is a reward never to be cut off." (95:4-6)

The last words clearly refer to the higher life which is never to be cut off. It cannot be that the whole of creation should serve a purpose and that man alone who is Lord of it and endowed with capabilities for ruling the universe should have a purposeless existence. Man has a higher object to fulfill; he has a higher life to live beyond this world; which is the real aim of human life in this world. The other argument which is given by *The Quran* in support of the resurrection is that good and evil must be given their reward and punishment respectively. Of all the living creations man alone has the power to discriminate between good and evil. *Allah* says in *The Quran*:

> "*Allah* wastes not the reward of the doers of good." (11:115, 12:90)

Allah again says in *The Quran*:

"As to those who believe and work righteousness, verily we shall not suffer to perish the reward of any who do a single righteous deed." (18:30)

The Quran continues:

"I will not suffer the work of any worker among you to be lost, whether male or female, the one of you being from the other." (3:194)

It is further said:

"So he who does an atom's weight of good, will see it. And he who does an atom's weight of evil, will see it." (99:7-8)

Such are some of the plain declarations made by *The Quran.* And when we look at nature around us we find the same law at work. Every cause has its effect and everything done must bear a fruit. Why should man's good or evil deed be an exception to this general rule working in the whole universe? And if they are not an exception as they should not be, the conclusion is evident that good and evil must bear their full fruit in another life, which indicate the continuity of the life of man in another world when death has put an end to it in this.

From the above discussion, it can be seen that the resurrection is not a dogma in which a man is required to believe for his salvation in another life rather it is a principle of human life, a principle which makes human life more serious and more useful while at the same time awakening in him the consciousness of a life that is higher. The man who sincerely believes in the resurrection will try his utmost to take advantage of every opportunity that is offered to him to live his life to the best purpose. He will try hard to do any good that he possibly can to the creatures of God and he will shun every evil deed as far as he can. Thus, a belief in the resurrection is needed in the first place to make his lower life worth living.

Without such a belief life looses not only its meaning, leaving man without any real and abiding aim, but also all incentives to do well and eschew evil.

Another question connected with the resurrection is whether it would be a corporeal resurrection. So far as our present experience goes, it is through the body that the spirit receives all its impressions of pleasure and pain that it gets knowledge and perception of things. Also, the impulses and sentiments of human beings are developed through body alone. According to the present state of our knowledge we cannot conceive of the soul without a body. But whether the soul in resurrection will receive back the same body which is left in this world is another question. There is nothing in *The Quran* to show that the body which the soul left at the time of death will be restored to it. On the other hand, there are statements to show that it will be a new creation and this body will be a spiritual body. To understand how this body is prepared, one must turn to *The Quran*. It is stated in *The Quran* that angels have been appointed to record the good and evil deeds of men. This concept is mentioned in *The Quran* as well as in Tradition. *Allah* mentions it in *The Quran*:

> "On that day you will see the faithful men and the faithful women, their light gleaming before them and on their right hand." (57:12)

It means that in the darkness of the Day of Judgment there will be a light to guide the righteous to their destination. This will be the light of their faith and their good works. Perhaps the light of the right hand mentioned here is the light of their good works because the blessed will receive their record in their right hand.[14]

The spiritual blindness of this life turns into blindness in the next life. As *Allah* says in *The Quran*:

> "Those who were blind in this world will be blind in the hereafter and most astray from the path." (17:72)

---

[14] *Ibid.*, Ref. 5288, p. 1500.

On the Judgment Day, the children of light will receive their reward and will render joyful thanks to God for His mercies. The children of darkness who had already been blind in this worldly life will not receive the light of God's mercy then. On the contrary, they will find that the longer the time they have travelled, the farther away they have gone from the right path.

The life after death takes two forms. In the first one is a life in paradise for those in whom the good exceeds the evil. The second one is a life in Hell for those in whom the evil exceeds the good. In *The Quran* the word paradise (*Firdaus*) occurs only twice. On the first occasion it is mentioned in *The Quran* in the following verse in conjunction with garden:

> "As to those who believe and work righteous deeds, they have for their entertainment the garden of paradise." (18:107)

On the second occasion it is mentioned in *The Quran*:

> "Those who faithfully observe their trust and their covenants and who guard their prayers those will be the heirs who will inherit paradise and they will dwell therein forever." (23:8-11)

The ultimate object of human being is described as meeting with God.

Allah says in *The Quran*:

> "O man! You must strive hard towards your Lord until you meet Him." (84:6)

But this object cannot be fully attained in this life. It is only in the life after death, the higher life, that man is able to reach this stage. Hence, it is that those who deny the life after death are said to be denier of the meeting with God. To be content with this life and not to look forward to a higher goal and a higher life is repeatedly condemned in *The Quran*. As it is said:

> "Those who rest not their hope on their meeting with us but are pleased and satisfied with the present life and do not pay heed to our signs, their abode is the fire (hell) because of the evil they earn." (10:7-8)

This verse says that those who fall from grace are described by three epithets: (1) the meeting with God is not the object of their hope and earnest desire but something else, (2) the material good of this world which not only attracts them but apparently gives them complete satisfaction so that there is no glow of the future in their horizon, and (3) they are deaf and dead to the resounding and do not messages of God. (1) and (2) refer to the extinction of faith in them and (3) to their failing a prey to the evils of this world in their conduct.[15]

---

15 *Ibid.*, Ref. 1395, p. 485.

The meeting with the Lord is one of the greatest goal to attain for which all good deeds are done. It is said in *The Quran*:

> "Whoever hopes to meet his Lord, he should do good deeds and join no one in the service of his Lord." (18:110)

The new life granted to the righteous in paradise is the starting-point for a new advancement in which man shall continue to rise to higher and higher places. Nor shall man ever grow weary in the attainment of these high stages of which even a conception cannot be formed. The joys of paradise are thus the true joys of advancement. People who will not get place in paradise will be thrown into the hell-fire. The different names of hell convey three different ideas, the idea of falling down to a great depth, the idea of burning and the idea of being broken down. Thus, the idea of rising higher and higher is connected with paradise that of falling down in depth is connected with Hell. The ideas of contentment and happiness are associated with paradise and the idea of burning is associated with paradise. All this is the result of man's own deeds because he follows his low desires and baser passions that make him fall into the abyss. The desires and passions for worldly objects changes into hell fire after death. The question, 'What is Hell'? is unequivocally discussed in *The Quran*:

> "The fire kindled by *Allah* which rises over the hearts." (104:6-7)

Hell, therefore, only represents the evil consequences of evil deeds but still it is not a place merely for undergoing the consequences of what has been done. It is also a remedial plan. Its chastisement is not for the purpose of torture but for purification, so that man can get rid of the evil consequences which he has brought about with his own hands, and may be made fit for spiritual advancement. Purification being the great object, the man who has wasted his opportunity here must undergo the ordeal of hell in order to obtain it.

The whole of the religion of Islam is briefly summed up in the two short sentences, *La ilaha ill-Allah* i.e. there is no God but *Allah,* or, nothing deserves to be made an object of love and worship except *Allah,* and *Muhammad-un Rasulullah,* Muhammad is the messenger of *Allah.* The first part of the creed is the constant theme of *The Quran,* and a faith in the Unity of God, is repeatedly mentioned as the basic principle not only of Islam but of every religion revealed by God. The second part, *'Muhammad-ur-Rasulul-allah'* occurs in *The Quran* which unambiguously states:

"Muhammad is the Apostle of God." (48:29)

The Quran again and again makes it clear that it is only in relation to these six grounds that faith is required. There is a slight variation in the *Hadith*:

"That you believe *in Allah* and *His Angels* and in the meeting with Him and *His Messengers* and you believe in the life after death." (*Al-Bukhari*, 2:37)

In *Hadith*, the books are not mentioned distinctly and are included in the word Messengers. Therefore, the basis of belief rests on six principles, according to *The Quran* and the Tradition: God, His Angels, His Prophets, His Books, Predestination and a Life after death.

All articles of faith are in reality principles of action. *Allah* as a Being possesses all the perfect qualities and when man is required to believe in *Allah*, he is required to make himself possessor of the highest moral qualities. Belief in the angels means that the believers should follow the good impulses which are inherent in him because the angels are the beings who prompt the doing of good. Belief in the books means that we should follow the directions contained in them for the development of inner faculties. Belief in Prophets means that they are our role-model and we have to shape our personality according to them and sacrifice our life for humanity as they did. Belief in the Hereafter means that physical advancement or material is not the end or goal of life. But its real purpose is a higher spiritual life of which the resurrection is but the beginning.

* * *

CHAPTER-III

EXPLICATION OF IQBAL'S PHILOSOPHY AND ITS APPLICATION TO THE INTERPRETATION AND ANALYSIS OF RELIGIOUS BELIEF

> Khudi kya hai? Raz-e-durun-e-hayat
> Khudi kya hai? Bedariye kaynat.
> (What is self? A secret in the life span
> What is self? Awareness about the universe.)
>
> – Mohd. Iqbal, *Bal-e-Jibreel*

> Wisdom is passionless. But faith by contrast is
> What Kierkegard calls a passion.
>
> – Ludwig Wittgenstein, *Culture and Value*

Mohammad Iqbal is one of the most important philosophers of the Islamic world. His writings – poetry and prose – are a source of inspiration for many. All his writings besides being profound are written in a simple lucid language which is comprehensible both to experts as well as lay man. They delight the reader. Among his other writings, his interpretation of *The Quran* is regarded as authentic by one and all. His narration and evaluation of the life of the Prophet is remarkable.

Iqbal, however, was not a philosopher in the sense of a system-builder like Plato. He never purported to give a system of thought, although there is a complete system in his thought. Iqbal's thought has a unique combination of Muslim philosopher's like Al-Ghazali and Rumi and Western Philosophers like Kant, Neitzsche and Russell. Like Al-Ghazali and Kant, he is aware of the limitations of reason. He in company with Rumi recognizes the limitations of reason but accepts its importance as a source of knowledge. However, unlike Freud and Russell, Iqbal does not agree that the salvation of man lies in reason. Reason is a means not an end. According to him, over-rationalism and excessive intellectualism have engendered materialism and atheism. The West has lost the 'inner spark', the 'restless soul' because of over-intellectualism and its heart is dead. He says that the East also by following the West has lost that inner spark, that fraternity, that faith which is the very spirit of Islamic teaching.

According to Iqbal, religion is not only a body of dogmas or rituals but a form of experience which ensures a grasp of nothing short of a direct and immediate illumination of the very core of reality also. It is what Wittgenstein would call, as we shall see later, a form of life. Along with religious experience he also recognizes the importance of other experiences as a necessary stage to realize the fullest possible insight into the ultimate nature of the real and towards spiritual enhancement of man. Iqbal holds that the religious experience is not discontinuous with other levels of experience. To him knowledge is not taken for its own sake. It is rather a means for establishing connection with the reality that confronts us, for it is on the establishment of this connection that both life and the outward march of the spirit of man depend. In the case of ordinary knowledge Iqbal would agree with Western epistemologists like Kant, who affirms that "knowledge is sense-perception elaborated by understanding."[1]

Further, he acknowledges that "it is with the weapon of this conceptual knowledge that man approaches the observable aspect of reality. The one noteworthy feature of *The Quran* is the emphasis that it lays on this observable aspect of reality."[2]

Here Iqbal is in agreement with Kant when he says that the concept of noumena as something is not knowable by the senses and is therefore, a limiting concept. You can know only phenomena i.e. appearance reality and the non-phenomenal, i.e. the noumenal, the intelligent is beyond you.[3] Commenting on this aspect of Kant's epistemology Iqbal says, "His critique of pure reason revealed the limitations of human reason and reduced the whole work of the rationalists to a heap of ruins. And justly has he been described as God's greatest gift to his country."[4] Iqbal acknowledges the importance of sense perception and reason, but besides these these two he also accepts the role of intuition in the attainment of fullest knowledge of reality. On Iqbal's view, Dr. Jamila Khatoon writes in her book, "In Iqbal's view, sense-perception, reason and intuition all are combined in an organic

---

1 M. Iqbal, *The Reconstruction of Religious Thought in Islam,* op. cit., p. 13.

2 *Ibid.,* p. 14.

3 Frank Thilly, *A History of Philosophy*, SBW Publisher, New Delhi, 2003, p. 407.

4 M. Iqbal, *The Reconstruction of Religious Thought in Islam*, op. cit., p. 5.

whole. He knew fully well that light from one direction alone could not illumine the whole of reality in all its manifestation and Iqbal cannot be classed under any of the three schools of philosophical thought i.e. the empiricist, rationalist or intuitionist."[5]

The Quran and the *Hadith* of Prophet Muhammad are the main source of inspiration for M. Iqbal. He believes in the fact that man can realize fully his potentialities only through abiding by the commandment of Almighty and following the illustrious example of the Holy Prophet in all aspects of life. He realized that the revival of man is possible only through the ultimate central principle of his being i.e. the self or ego. According to Iqbal, self is the most comprehensive principle of life and universe and all movements including theoretical and practical originate in it. Iqbal is essentially known as a religious philosopher. Therefore, in this chapter I would cover the famous philosophical topics like God, universe and the self the well-known trinity of Iqbal's philosophy.

GOD: The concept of God dominates the whole thought of Iqbal and permeates his entire system. His faith in the existence of God is based on the testimony of *The Quran* and the mystic literature of Islam. The latest discourses of modern science in the domain of Physics and Biology have

[5] Jamila Khatoon, *The Place of God, Man and Universe in the Philosophic System of Iqbal*, Iqbal Academy Pakistan, Lahore, 1963, P. 3.

also strengthened his faith. According to Iqbal, God is the most real, the final and ultimate being, as the self-subsisting, primordial and necessary existence. God, to him, is the source of all existence, and fountainhead of matter, space, time, of the complexities of life and mind, of system, organization and harmony. He is the Supreme Ego, the Supreme Self and Perfect Personal Individuality.

God is invisible as we cannot see him with our eyes and cannot form an adequate conception of him. He is visible in so far as we can mark his imprints in the visible aspects of nature, and see Him with the eyes of our heart. According to *The Quran,* there are signs of the existence of God for those who try to understand it. *Allah* says in *The Quran*:

"He is one who causes life and who causes death and to him belong the alternation of day and night. Why do you not understand them?"(23:80)

Iqbal, like Bergson, reaches the conception of Ultimate Reality through immediate experience or intuition. According to him, the perception or the observation of what is external and related to the efficient self cannot give the valid, profound and immediate knowledge of Ultimate Reality. It is only when we turn our gaze within that Ultimate Reality that its full and naked glory dawns upon us. The perception of things that confront us in the outer world is superficial and external, but the perception of one's own self is internal, intimate and profound. Conscious experience establishes one's absolute contact with Reality and an analysis of this state may make the ultimate meaning of existence clear.[6]

Iqbal believes in the Personal God and he defends his position with the Quranic idea of Divine Reality. *The Quran* describes God as the light of the heavens and the earth, which led many thinkers to interpret God as an impersonal cosmic reality, immanent in the world and not transcendent to it. Iqbal tried to refute this interpretation as wrong and misleading and uses a metaphor in favour of his position.

He quotes from *The Quran,* "God is the light of the Heaven and of the earth. His light is like a niche in which is a lamp-the lamp encased in a glass-the glass, as it were, a star." (24:35)

No doubt, the opening sentence of the verse gives the impression of an escape from an individualistic conception of God. But when we follow the metaphor of light in the rest of the verse, it gives just the opposite impression. The development of the metaphor is meant rather to exclude the suggestion of a formless cosmic element by centralizing the light in a flame which is further individualized by its encasement in a glass likened

6 M. Iqbal, *The Reconstruction of Religious Thought in Islam*, op. cit., p. 48.

unto a well-defined star.[7] He points out that the metaphor of light is not meant to suggest the omnipresence of God. According to modern physicists, light is the same in its velocity to all observers irrespective of their own system of movement. Thus, in the world of change, light is the nearest approach to the Absolute. The metaphor of light as applied to God, therefore, in view of modern knowledge, must be taken to suggest the Absoluteness of God and not His Omnipresence which easily lends itself to a pantheistic interpretation.[8] Here, Iqbal defends and explains *The Quran's* conception of personal and individual God. He elucidates his own position and tries to establish it on a firm and solid ground.

Creativeness is one of the most important attributes of Godhead. God is not identified with great cosmos. He is not the substance of Spinoza that is presented as the Ultimate, Necessary, Self-determined and free-cause from whose external necessity of nature the infinite number of things necessarily flows or continually follows, in the same way as it follows from the very nature of a triangle that its three angles are equal to two right angles.[9] The whole reality according to Iqbal is the outcome of God's consciousness and purposive activity as is related to the universe as a creator to his creation. But

---

7 *Ibid.*, p. 64.

8 *Ibid.*, p. 65.

9 Frank Thilly, *A History of Philosophy*, op. cit., p. 295.

this does not mean that He is related to His creation as a pot-maker is related to his pot. If he is thus identified, He will be brought down to the finite level and will be reduced to a finite personality limited and restricted by external environment and circumstances. All the meaningless theological controversies about the idea of creation arise from this narrow vision of finite mind. Thus regarded the universe is a mere accident in the life of God and might not have been created.[10]

God, according to Iqbal is Almighty, All-powerful and Omnipotent but His omnipotence and power is not blind and unpredictable. If omnipotence is not reconciled with limitation, it cannot be attributed or applied to Divine Reality. Iqbal says in his book,

> "*The Quran* has no liking for abstract universals. It always fixes its gaze on the concrete which the theory of relativity has only recently taught modern philosophy to see. All activity creational or otherwise is a kind of limitation without which it is impossible to conceive God as a concrete operative Ego."[11]

God is omnipotent but at the same time He is wise and good also. Divine will is rationally directed and is also characterized with goodness.

---

10 M. Iqbal, *The Reconstruction of Religious Thought in Islam*, op. cit., p. 66.

11 *Ibid.*, p. 81.

Divine wisdom and Divine goodness put a limit upon Divine Omnipotence and power. Iqbal further says,

> "Omnipotence, abstractly conceived, is merely a blind, capricious power without limits. *The Quran* has a clear and definite conception of nature as a cosmos of mutually related forces. *The Quran*, therefore, views Divine Omnipotence as intimately related with the Divine wisdom and finds the infinite power of God revealed, not in the arbitrary and the capricious but in the recurrent, the regular and the orderly."[12]

God, according to Iqbal, is Eternal, Dynamic Will, External Beauty, Eternal light and so on. He has no beginning, no end and is over and above temporal and spatial order. According to Iqbal, time and space do not exist as external to and independent of God. They are rather the outcome of Divine creative activity. Here, he agrees with Mir Damad and Mulla Baqar as they say, "Time is born with the act of creation by which the ultimate ego realizes and measures, so to speak, the infinite wealth of His own undermined creative possibilities."[13]

The above discussion shows that the concept of God in Iqbal's philosophy is over and above the serial time and space but this does not

---

[12] *Ibid*, p. 81.

[13] *Ibid.*, p. 78.

show that God is an immovable and unchangeable entity whose perfection is entirely irreconcilable with the conception of change or flux. God is dynamic and cannot be conceived as static reality whose perfection is disturbed even by the slightest idea of movement. Iqbal says that if perfection is without change then it will render God as a closed system with no possibility of novelty and spontaneity and this idea will deprive Him of His free-will. He brings out compromise between eternity, change, and conscious perfection to be a synthesis of both. He applies all the three attributes to God. God changes and moves but without succession and thus comprehends in Himself change with permanence.

According to Iqbal, another very important passage for contact between God and man is prayer. The act of prayer as aiming at knowledge resembles reflection. Yet prayer at its highest is much more than abstract reflection. Like reflection, it too is a process of assimilation, but the assimilative process in the case of prayer draws itself closely together and thereby acquires a power unknown to pure thought. In thought the mind observes and follows the working of Reality. In the act of prayer it gives up its career as a seeker of slow-footed universality and rises higher than thought to capture reality itself with a view to become a conscious participator in its life. There is nothing mystical about it. Prayer as a means of spiritual illumination is a normal vital act by which the little island of our personality suddenly discovers its situation in a larger whole of life.[14] But Iqbal's concept of prayer is different from anthropologist and pantheistic conception of prayer. An anthropologist worshipper prostrates himself before supra-mundane and extramundane reality, which is beyond and above, external and unrelated to His creation and is empowered to intervene and is capable of bringing changes in what He has created and pre-ordained to His creatures. On the other hand, according to pantheistic worshipper, prayer is an inner state of soul having its direct effect on the soul. Pantheistic God is immanent and extramundane reality and the change in the permanent and natural order of events through prayer is inconceivable and absurd. But Iqbal's position is somewhat different from both the views. God, to him, is transcendent and even immanent. He is organically related to the finite self and at the same time is beyond and above it. The meaning and significance of prayer also changes accordingly. In the act of prayer man is dynamically and organically related to Divine reality. But prayer is not merely a state of soul having its effect on the world soul because of the organic relation of the finite soul with the infinite. It is also a contact between Divine personality and human personality and the former is related to the latter not like a whole to its parts but as the creator to the created and

14 *Ibid.*, pp. 90-91.

is immanent and transcendent to it. In this act of prayer man comes into personal relation with God.

Universe: Regarding the creation of the universe various metaphysical theories present different views. The Greek atomist, the dualistic and Western philosophers of science till 19th century presented a materialistic explanation of the universe. The atoms are permanent and indivisible entities with no intrinsic and qualitative distinctions. Atoms are different only quantitatively and are determined geometrically by their form, position and arrangement. And the universe comes into existence because of their combination, arrangement and rearrangement.

Iqbal takes the help of *The Quran* and quotes a verse from it to show that the creation of the world is not the result of a mere creative sport of the creator:

> "We have not created the Heavens and the Earth and whatever is between them, in sport. We have not created them but for a serious end. But most of them do not understand." (44:38-39)

This verse of *The Quran* clearly says that all creation is for a wise and just purpose. But men usually do not realize or understand it because they are steeped in their own ignorance, folly or passion. Iqbal rejects all those theories which takes world in negative terms and accept the world as unreal, illusory or Maya.

Allah further says in *The Quran*:

> "Verily in the creation of the heaven and of the earth, and in the succession of the night and of the day are signs for the men of understanding; who, standing and sitting and reclining, bear God in mind and reflect on the creation of the heavens and of the earth and say, Oh, our Lord! Thou have not created this in vain." (3:190-191)

Iqbal criticized Plato and those thinkers who accept this world as a super sensuous world and denounce this world of sense-experience.

This world and the object of this world cannot be rejected as false or unreal. Iqbal is a monist and was fully aware of the weaknesses, contradictions and inconsistencies of dualism which create a gulf between the Divine Reality and the visible existence, between spirit and matter, between soul and body. In his criticism of the theological argument, he tries to explode the conception of design in nature or deistic theology and the dualistic interpretation of reality. He traces the whole 'wonderland' of matter, life and mind to one fountainhead, to one supreme source. He banishes the gulf between God as creator and the universe as created.[15]

[15] Jamila Khatoon, *The Place of God, Man and Universe in the Philosophic System of Iqbal*, op. cit., p. 79.

Let us first turn our attention to matter. In order exactly to appreciate the position of modern Physics it is necessary to understand clearly what we mean by matter. Physics, as an empirical science, deals with the facts of experience, i.e. sense-experience. The physicist begins and ends with the sensible phenomena, without which it is impossible for him to verify his theories. He may postulate imperceptible entities, such as atoms but he does so because he cannot otherwise explain his sense-experience. Thus, Physics studies the material world i.e. the world revealed by the senses. The mental processes involved in this study and similarly religious and aesthetic experience, though part of the total range of experience are excluded from the scope of Physics for the obvious reason that Physics is restricted to the study of the material world by which we mean the world of things we perceive.[16]

But what are the things we perceive in the material world? When it is asked what we exactly perceive of these things, the answer is its qualities. In sky, mountain, chair, etc. we may easily point out certain qualities which we observe. Thus, a distinction is drawn between a thing and its qualities.

By following the empirical approach, Locke said that it is through sense-experience that we collect all the material of the knowledge of the external

---

16 *The Reconstruction of Religious Thought in Islam,* op. cit., p. 33.

world. He draws a distinction between a thing and its qualities and admits two sorts of qualities, primary and secondary. The primary qualities belong to the objects themselves and are utterly inseparable from them such are: solidity, extension, figure, motion or rest and number. The secondary qualities are nothing in the object themselves but power to produce various sensations in us by their primary qualities such as colours, sounds, tastes etc.[17]

Berkeley was a highly religious person and because of this he rejected the Locke's theory of matter. Iqbal says, "It was the philosopher Berkley who first undertook to refute the theory of matter as the unknown cause of sensation."[18] Thus, according to him, the universe is not explicable or intelligible apart from the Ultimate Ego. Iqbal agrees with Berkley when he refutes the theory of matter as the solid substance and unknown and unknowable substratum underlying the visible and tangible reality and being the unknown cause of our sensations. According to this theory, as presented by Locke and his followers, perceptions and illusion do not disclose nature in its real and genuine essence. But this cause lies in matter or material things which, as unverifiable and imperceptible entities, produce them.[19] To understand the nature of the world through empirical means does not appeal

[17] Frank Thilly, *A History of Philosophy,* op. cit., p. 311.

[18] *The Reconstruction of Religious Thought in Islam,* op. cit., p. 34.

[19] *The Place of God, Man and Universe in the Philosophical System of Iqbal,* op. cit., p. 84.

to Iqbal. He is not a mere empiricist or rationalist or intuitionist. In his philosophy, sense-perception, reason and intuition are given their proper places but intuition is regarded as the highest form of knowledge. He says that sense-experience gives us only a superficial knowledge of a thing and does not give a proper understanding of the world.

Iqbal upholds the view that every culture represents some sort of naturalism which is peculiar to its own world-feeling which further ends in some sort of atomism. So, we have the examples of Indian atomism, Greek atomism, Muslim atomism and modern atomism. The Islamic atomism, therefore, presents one of the most interesting chapters in the history of Muslim culture. According to Ash'arite, this universe is composed of infinitely small atoms which cannot be further divided. *The Quran* says that the universe is so constituted that it is capable of extension. As it is said in *The Quran*:

> "He (God) adds to the creation as He pleases because He has power over all things." (35:1)

It means it is not a block universe, a finished product, immobile and incapable of change. Deep in its inner being lies, perhaps, the dream of a new birth. Iqbal rejects the *Ash'arite* theory of creation which supports the doctrine of accident by saying that it is a kind of materialism. However, he supports the *Ash'arite* when they say that nothing has a stable nature. Iqbal appreciated the *Ash'arite* theory of continuous creation.

Iqbal points out that Prof. Whitehead is right in holding the view that,

> "Nature is not a static fact situated in an a-dynamic void, but a structure of events possessing the character of a continuous creative flow which thought cuts up into isolated immobility's out of whose mutual relations arise the concepts of space and time. Thus we see how modern science utters its agreement with Berkley's criticism which it once regarded as an attack on its very foundation."[20]

Iqbal says that the recent discoveries in the field of science have strengthened my faith in spiritualism and the traditional notion of materialism has been totally rejected. Iqbal would, therefore, believe that the ultimate character of reality is spiritual. Reality, according to him, is essential spirit. But of course there are degrees of spirit. Thus, we can say that he believes in the degrees of reality. But he is not the first thinker to accept this. In the Islamic philosophy the concept of degrees of reality appears in the writings of Shahabuddin Saharwardi. In the Western philosophy, this idea was worked out by Leibnitz, Hegel, and many modern neo-Hegelians, though their treatment is quite different from that of Iqbal.

---

[20] *The Reconstruction of Religious Thought in Islam*, op. cit. p. 35.

Iqbal said that there is a gradual rising of the ego until it reaches perfection in man as *The Quran* declares that ultimate ego is nearer to man. Iqbal conceives this universe as an ego and on the line of our conscious experience he says, that the universe is a free creative movement. Therefore, the three important aspects of this universe are freedom, creativity and movement. As the world is creative so its movement is not taking place according to a fixed plan. As Iqbal says,

> "What we call things is events in the continuity of nature which thought spatializes and thus regards as mutually isolated for purpose of action. The universe which seems to us to be a collection of things is not a solid stuff occupying a void. It is not a thing but an act."[21]

Iqbal's universe is the real creation of Divine Reality and it is created without an instrumentality foreign to it. God creates the universe out of his own being. It does not come by God's word of power out of nothing. Creation out of nothing gives nothing *'ex nihilo nihil fit'*. Like many other theists, Iqbal did not merely believe in the theory of creation. According to him, creation takes the form of evolution but it cannot be conclusively said that when did creation start.

---

[21] *Ibid.*, p. 49.

SELF: The problem of the self is the central problem in the philosophy of Mohammad Iqbal. He calls it with various names like *'Khudi'*, selfhood, individuality and personality. The problem of self is the basic problem in his poetic work *'Asrar-i-Khudi'*[22] (The secret of the self) which was first published at Lahore in 1915.

In his refutation of 'the Self', Iqbal starts by saying that the whole reality in its ultimate essence is spirit (ego). He accepts the Quranic view according to which ego emerges within the spatio-temporal order out of fine clay. God created man and at the same time he evolves out of matter. Life emerges from matter gradually, with unicellular organism as its first manifestation and with man as its crowning and highest masterpiece placed at the top of the ladder. But this matter is not the same matter presented by materialists. It is the not-self that is posited by the Ultimate Ego or the ultimate self in order to reveal and manifest him.[23]

To explain the creation of human ego and its emergence in the space and time Iqbal takes the help of *The Quran*. As *Allah* says in *The Quran*:

> "We created man from a quintessence of clay; then placed him as sperm in a place of rest; then made sperm into a clot of congealed

---

22 Mohd. Iqbal, *The Secret of the Self (Asrar-i-Khudi),* trans. Reynold A Nicholson, Kitab Bhavan, New Delhi, 2004.

23 Mohd. Iqbal, *Asrar-o-Ramooz*, Lahore: trans. Sh. Ghulam Ali, 1975, p. 12.

blood; then changed that clot into a foetus; then changed that foetus into bones with flesh; then we developed out of it another creature. So, blessed be God, the best to create." (23:12-14)

The emergence of human ego has gone through a process of change and transformation. The idea of evolution is perfectly consistent with the teaching of *The Quran*. As Iqbal says, "According to *The Quran*, man is not a stranger on this earth, and *Allah* says, that we have caused you to grow from the earth."[24]

The soul or ego or self derives its existence from God or the Ultimate Ego. It emerges out of sub-egos when their interaction and association teach a certain level of coordination. At this point self-consciousness, the feeling of ego-hood, manifests itself. The will that assumes the form of sub-egos, manifest itself in the higher egos or finite individuals. At this level, the mental which at the lower level was dominated by the physical, rises to the position of dominance and greater independence. Here we have the emergence of the level at which the Ultimate Reality reveals its secret and furnishes a clue to its ultimate nature.[25] The soul is not a simple, indivisible and immutable substance as it is defined by Al-Ghazali. It is not a receptacle or substratum in which mental states are inhered. Iqbal rejects

---

[24] *The Reconstruction of Religious Thought in Islam,* op. cit., p. 80.

[25] *Ibid.*, p. 106.

this conception of the soul and agrees with the objection of Kant to the conception of soul as a metaphysical entity. Kant points out 'I think' accompanies every thought and is only the formal condition of thought to the ontological substance and here is committed a logical mistake. Further, Kant asserts that indestructibility of the substance cannot be logically inferred from its individuality.[26]

Iqbal's concept of the self is somewhat similar to the modern philosopher Descartes. The object of Descartes was to apply mathematical method of philosophy to obtain certitude in knowledge and that knowledge he got as *Cogito Ergo Sum* means 'I think therefore I am'. He says, you can doubt everything but you cannot doubt the fact that you are thinking right now. This is self-evident truth. According to Descartes, *Cogito ergo sum* is the one certain truth which may be taken as the foundation of philosophy. So by this principle he tries to establish the existence of the self. Both Descartes and Iqbal believed in the existence of the self on the basis of intuition. But the meaning of intuition is not always same for both. In Descartes, intuition is logical, intellectual and rational. For Iqbal, it is of the nature of love, poetic and illuminating. Descartes said that the self is that which thinks, a thing that doubts, that understands, affirms, denies, wills,

---

[26] *Ibid.*, p. 101.

refines, that imagines and perceives and its principle attribute is thought but Iqbal like Descartes does not believe that its principle attribute is thought.

According to the *Ash'arite* school of thinkers, the world is compounded of what they call *'Jawahir'*, infinitely small parts or atoms which cannot be further divided. Since the creative activity of God is ceaseless, the number of the atoms cannot be finite. Fresh atoms are coming into being every moment and the universe is constantly growing. As *The Quran* says, 'God adds to His creation what He wills.' The essence of the atom is independent of its existence. This means that existence is a quality imposed on the atoms by God.[27]

The famous Muslim theologian Al-Ghazali said in this regard that the self is simple, indivisible and immutable. The self perceives things. But perception as an attribute can exist only in a substance which is absolutely free from all the attributes of body. In his book, *Al-Madnun,* Al-Ghazali explains why Prophet declined to reveal the nature of the soul. He says that there are two kinds of men; ordinary men and thinkers. The former, who look upon materiality as a condition of existence, cannot conceive an immaterial substance. The latter are led, by their logic, to a conception of the soul which sweeps away all difference between God and the individual

---

27 *Ibid.*, p. 69.

soul. He, therefore, realized the pantheistic drift of his inquiry and preferred silence as to the ultimate nature of the soul.[28]

Iqbal further says that whatever be the characteristic of the ego it reveals itself as a unity in what we call mental states. Mental states do not exist in mutual isolation. They mean and involve one another. It fundamentally differs from the unity of material things, for the parts of material things can exist in mutual isolation. Mental unity is absolutely unique.[29] The self, according to him has two parts – the appreciative and the efficient. To feel the inner secret and mystery of life and the universe is the function of appreciative self. But on the other hand, the efficient self acts upon the external environment. This self is our practical self and is the subject-matter of psychology. It is known only in moments of profound meditation and contemplation.

Now I will take up the issue of relationship between soul and body as discussed by Iqbal. In modern philosophy this issue of relationship between soul and body was discussed by Descartes and Spinoza in great detail. According to Descartes, mind is diametrically opposed to body. The attribute of body is extension. The body is passive, mind is active. The two

---

28 M. Iqbal, *The Development of Metaphysics in Persia*, Bazm-I-Iqbal, Lahore, 1900, p. 60.

29 *The Reconstruction of Religious Thought in Islam*, op. cit. p. 93.

are absolutely distinct from each other. We cannot conceive of mind or soul without thought. He tells us in his *Discourse on Method* that a thinking thing is one that doubts, understands, conceives, affirms, denies, wills, refuses, imagines, as well as feels. Regarding the interaction between the two Descartes accepts the theory of causal interaction. The soul, though united with the whole body, has its principle seat in the pineal gland of the brain and through that gland a certain interaction between mind and body takes place. But Descartes does not succeed in showing how this interaction is compatible with his metaphysical dualism of thinking and extended substance.[30] The probable location pointed out by him is the 'pineal gland' otherwise there is no common characteristic between soul and body.

Spinoza, being a pantheist, accepts that there is one and the only one substance and this single, eternal, infinite, self-caused and necessary principle of things is called God or nature. God and the world are one. It is self-caused, *causa-sui*, because if it were produced by anything else, it would be dependent on that. Substance, of Spinoza, consists of infinite number of attributes, and of these the mind can grasp only two. Nature expresses itself in an infinite number of ways, of which only extension and thought are knowable by man who is himself physical and mental

[30] Frank Thilly, *A History of Philosophy*, op. cit., p. 208.

beings.[31] Spinoza destroys the substantial dualism of the universe found in Descartes philosophy and establishes the philosophy of monism by saying that soul and body are inseparable attributes of one and the same substance. Iqbal does not support the theory of causal interaction enunciated by Descartes. He rejects dualism by saying that nature does not bifurcate itself into the mental and the physical. But Iqbal's theory is closer to Spinoza's theory of mind and matter. Both accept mind and matter as inseparable entities. They are the manifestation of one reality. But the difference between Iqbal and Spinoza lies in that Spinoza is 'Pantheist' and Iqbal a 'Monotheist'. The other problem in Spinoza's philosophy is the problem of reconciliation between the theory of substance and attribute. The other difficulty in his system is that his philosophy violates the law of contradiction since how the same substance can be extended and thinking at the same time.

Iqbal rejects theory of 'Parallelism' given by Spinoza as well as theory of 'Interactionism' given by Descartes. He rejects parallelism altogether because in any form it reduces soul to a mere passive spectator of the happenings of the body. He says, "It is quite useless to retain the soul as a passive spectator or as an unnecessary appendage. By rejecting

---

[31] *Ibid.*, p. 215.

'Interactionism', he says we have no observable facts at own disposal to show where exactly their interaction takes place and which of the two takes the initiative. Because of this limitation the power of initiative may be attributed to any of the two while reducing the other as a consenting partner. Here again the soul is liable to being reduced to a more secondary position."[32]

According to Iqbal, "There is no gulf between body and soul. Both are the expression of the same reality. The soul is a system of acts and so is the body. But the ego is spontaneous activity; the acts composing the body repeat themselves. The body is accumulated action or habit of the soul and as such non-detachable from it. It is the permanent element of conscious which in view of this permanent element appears from the outside as something stable."[33]

The view of Hume and William James about self is different from Iqbal. Hume denies the reality of the self as having some metaphysical entity because conscious experience gives no clue to it. Hume says, "When I enter most intimately into what I call myself, I always stumble on some particular perception or other, of heat or cold, light or shade, pain or

[32] *The Reconstruction of Religious Thought in Islam,* op. cit., p. 105.

[33] *Ibid.*, p. 106.

pleasure. I never catch myself at any time without a perception and can never observe anything but the perception."[34] According to Iqbal, Hume's study of the self is very limited. Our conscious experience, through a series of mental states, cannot reveal the depth of our personality. It is through intuition alone that one can go into its real nature.

According to William James, self is not a substance or entity. For him, the self which is 'pure self' is the principle of personal identity. It is a passing thought and the only thinker superimposed in some mysterious way is the brain. In short, we can say that the self for him has the characteristic of a thinker and not an object of thought. The ego, for him, is a flow or stream of thought and experiences.

Iqbal's concept of the self is much different from that of William James. For James self is nothing more than a thinker. It is a physical phenomena whereas according to Iqbal, the self is spiritual reality. He does not take it just as a thinker but as an 'aluminous point'. It has a permanent element though it is not an entity, substance or transcendental self. It is spiritual and precedes from 'Lord's *Amr* (command)', 'the directive energy of God.'[35]

---

[34] Frank Thilly, *A History of Philosophy,* op. cit., p. 355.

[35] *The Reconstruction of Religious Thought in Islam,* op. cit., p. 103.

According to Iqbal, self is not above the inner experience. He says, "I do not mean to say that the ego is over and above the mutually penetrating multiplicity we call experience. Inner experience is the ego at work. We appreciate the ego itself in the act of perceiving, judging, and willing. The life of the ego is a kind of tension caused by the ego invading the environment and environment invading the ego. The ego does not stand outside this arena of mutual invasion. It is present in it as directive energy and is formed and disciplined by its own experience."[36]

Iqbal bases his view on the Quranic verdict. He thinks that God is the ultimate ego from whom the finite egos precede. He says, "I have conceived the ultimate reality as an Ego; and I must add now that from the ultimate ego only egos proceed."[37] The self, according to him, is only command of *Allah,* which is above the understanding of human knowledge. In support of his argument he quotes the following from *The Quran*;

> "And they ask thee of the soul. Say: the soul proceeds from my Lord's command but of knowledge only a little is given to you." (17:87)

Iqbal believes in earned immortality and rejects the idea of transmigration of soul. By earned immorality he means that the immortality is

36 *Ibid.*, p. 105.

37 *Ibid.*, p. 71.

not the lot of every individual; it is earned through deeds. According to him, it is only the fully developed self which earns immortality. He further says that even *The Quran* is quite clear in its view of earned immortality. He quotes:

> "By the soul and He who has balanced it, and has shown to it the ways of wickedness and piety, blessed is he who has made it grown and undone is he who corrupted it." (91:7-10)

Regarding the transmigration of the soul he says that it is not accepted in *The Quran*. Because as *Allah* said in *The Quran*:

> "When the trumpet is blown, there will be no more relationship between them that day, nor will one ask after another. Those whose balance of good deed is heavy they will attain salvation and those whose balance is light will be those who have lost their souls and will rest in Hell."[38]

This verse of *The Quran* clearly says that the old relationship of the world will be dissolved. Each soul will stand on its own merits. Good and evil deeds will be weighed against each other. If the good deeds prevail, the soul will attain prosperity, well-being, bliss or salvation; if the contrary happens there will be the misery and anguish of hell.

* * *

---

[38] *Ibid.*, 23:101-103.

CHAPTER-IV
RELIGIOUS BELIEFS AND LANGUAGE-GAMES

> Yaqeen mohkam, amal paiham, mohabbat faatahey alam
> Jihad-e-zindagani men ye hai mardon ki shamsheeren.
> (Strong faith, continuous action, love which conquers the world
> These three are the swords of a brave person in the struggle of life.)
>
> – Mohd. Iqbal, *Bang-e-Dara*

> Religious similes can be said to move on the edge of an abyss.
>
> – Ludwig Wittgenstein, *Culture and Value*

So far, in the previous chapters, I have discussed the Islamic concept of religious beliefs as mentioned in *The Quran* and also interpreted it by one of the most important Islamic philosopher, Mohammad Iqbal. In this chapter, I propose to discuss the nature of religious beliefs in the context of language-game as propounded by the contemporary philosopher Ludwig Wittgenstein. His philosophy of religious beliefs is also guided by his later philosophy of language-games. According to this theory, to grasp the meaning of a word we have to understand the role that it plays in the language-game in which it is used.

Twentieth-century philosophy had been deeply and sharply conscious of the connection between philosophical problems and language. Although several philosophers like Bertrand Russell, G.E. Moore and A.J. Ayer contributed to this dramatic shift in the enterprise of philosophy, Ludwig Wittgenstein contributed so much to this line of thought that his work proved to be decisive to understand the connection between philosophy and language. His philosophy had two phases: earlier and later. In the later phase he had repudiated his earlier thought although the central issue remained the same, i.e., *language*. The philosophy in his earlier work, *Tractatus-Logico-Philosophicus*, was inadequate because it assumed that language has really only one function, namely, to state facts. More seriously, Wittgenstein had assumed that the skeleton of all language is a logical one. While later on, by the time of *Philosophical Investigations* (1953), he realized that language has *many* functions besides simply "picturing" objects. Language always functions in a *context* and therefore has as many purposes as there are contexts. In his view, words are like "tools in a tool-box; there is a hammer, pliers, a saw, a screw-driver, a rule, a glue-pot, glue, nails and screws. The function of the words is as diverse as the functions of these objects. Of course, what confuses us is the uniform appearance of words when we hear them spoken or meet them in script and print. For their application is not presented to us so clearly especially when we are doing philosophy."[1]

He further says:

> "We must do away with all *explanation*, and description alone must take its place. And this description gets its light, that is to say its purpose, from the philosophical problems. These are, of course, not

1 Ludwig Wittgenstein, *Philosophical Investigation,* Tran. G.E.M. Anscombe, Blackwell Publisher, 2001, § 11.

empirical problems; they are solved, rather, by looking into the workings of our language, and that in such a way as to make us recognize those workings: *in spite of* an urge to misunderstand them. The problems are solved, not by giving new information, but by arranging what we have always known. Philosophy is a battle against the bewitchment of our intelligence by means of language." (PI, 109)

Our incorrect picture of language is produced by grammatical illusions. After recognizing the diversity of the functions of language, Wittgenstein inevitably altered the task of philosophy. He moved away from what Russell and Carnap were doing and turned in the direction of G.E. Moore's earlier emphasis upon the analysis of ordinary language, testing it by the criterion of "common sense". Now Wittgenstein opined that language does not contain one single pattern alone, that it is as variable as life itself. Indeed, he said, "it is easy to imagine a language consisting only of orders and reports in battle or a language consisting only of questions and expressions for answering yes or no and innumerable others and to imagine a form of life". (PI, 19)

Therefore, analysis should consist not in the *definition* of language or its meaning but rather in a careful description. As Wittgenstein says, "We must do away with all explanation, and *description alone* must take its place". (PI, 11)

We must "stick to the subjects of everyday thinking, and not go astray and imagine that we have to describe extreme subtleties" (PI, 18). Confusion arises not when our language is "doing work", but only when it is "like an engine idling". Till this phase, it was simply assumed that all language, in spite of certain superficial differences, is alike, the way all games are alike. Wittgenstein uncovered the flaw in this analogy by taking the case of games and asking:

> "Consider for example the proceedings that we call "games". I mean board-games, card-games, ball-games, Olympic-games, and so on. What is common to them all? Don't say: There *must* be something common, or they would not be called 'games' — but *look and see* whether there is anything common at all. For if you look at them you will not see something that is common to all, but similarities, relationships, and a whole series of them at that. To repeat: don't think, but look". (PI, 66)

Because philosophical problems grow out of language, it is necessary to acquire a basic familiarity with the usages of the language out of which each problem arises. As there are many kinds of games, there are many sets of rules of the games. Similarly, as there are many forms of languages, there are many forms of ordinary language of work, play, worship, science and so forth, there are many *usages*. Under these circumstances, "the work of the philosopher consists in *assembling reminders* for a particular purpose." (PI, 127)

"The problems arising through a misinterpretation of our forms of language have deep character. They are deep disquietudes; their roots are as deep in us as the forms of our language and their significance is as great as the importance of our language." (PI, 51)

Philosophy was for him an *activity* and his aim in engaging in it were largely conceptually therapeutic, to help, as he put it, the purpose of philosophy -to show fly way out of the fly bottle. He carefully attended to our language as it was used in context and has remarkably finely attuned it. For him philosophical nonsense emerged largely from not properly understanding the workings of our language, particularly when we reflect about it in specific contexts. He saw language as an activity; we play various and diverse language games for various purposes. None of these language-games has priority over others, and there is no super-language or cluster of basic language-games on which all others depend; there is no foundational base which gives the rest their legitimacy or insures their rationality.

Wittgenstein utterly rejects such rationalism or foundationalism whether it is thought to be metaphysical or scientific. Such approaches do not attend to how language actually functions, but impose a picture on it. Our actual languages are constituted by language-games. These language-games are embedded in practices that human beings in a society characteristically engage in and that deeply form them.

Within a language-game there is typical justification and lack of justification, evidence and proof as well as mistaken and groundless opinion. But we can't say this for language-games, practices, and forms of life (modes of social life) themselves taken as a whole. That is to say, we cannot say of a language-game or practice (or a whole cluster of language-games or a form of life) that we have something that is justified or unjustified, something that is reasonable or unreasonable, something we have evidence for, proof for and the like. And we cannot say we lack any of these things either, for we do not understand what it would be like to have them. There is no coherent way even of saying they are reasonable or unreasonable. These applausive terms have no grip here.

"Beliefs, utterances, conceptions, concepts are only intelligible in the context of ways of living or modes of social life as such."[2] Science is one

---

[2] Winch, Peter. *Idea of a Social Science*, 2nd ed. London: Routledge, 1995, p.100-101.

such mode, morality another, and religion still another or perhaps they are each distinctive clusters of language-games and practices *in* a form of life. As Peter Winch says, 'Each has a criterion of intelligibility peculiar to itself... Within Science or religion actions can be logical or illogical', rational or irrational, justified or lacking in justification, reasonable or unreasonable, worthy of acceptance or not'.[3]

Judaism, Christianity, Islam, Buddhism, Hinduism are themselves either forms of life or *in* a given forms of life (depending on how we take Wittgenstein). Still, religious language-games with their practices, along with other language-games, are not Balkanized. How they are taken depends on their connections with other language-games. However, the religious language-games, as we have seen, still have their distinctive criteria and distinctive point. It is claimed that we cannot reasonably assess all our religious practices from outside because they are just there like our lives and they either mean something to us, have some importance to us or they do not.[4] Indeed, we cannot stand outside *all* practices and criticize anything; there is no practice-free perspective of anything.[5] But using one practice or

---

3 Winch, Peter, *Idea of a Social Science*, op. cit., p. 95.

4 Rhees, R. *Rush Rhees on Religion and Philosophy*, ed, D.Z. Phillips, Cambridge, 1997, p. 121.

5 Neilsen, K. and D.Z. Phillips, *Wittgensteinian Fideism?* London: SCM Press, 2005, p.95.

cluster of practices, we can sometimes relevantly criticize another practice or cluster of practices.[6]

Wittgenstein launched an attack on what has been called the *picture theory of meaning,* according to which statements may be judged true or false depending upon whether reality matches the picture represented by the belief or not. This understanding of truth and beliefs which is similar to the correspondence theory of truth in which the statement "God exists" is true if and only if God exists, seemed to Wittgenstein to be misguided. It gives rise to insoluble philosophical problems and it misses the whole point of having religious beliefs, which is that the meaning is to be found in the life in which they are employed. By shifting attention away from the referential meaning of words to their use, Wittgenstein promoted the idea that we should attend to what he called *forms of life.* As this move was applied to religious matters, a number of philosophers either denied or at least played down the extent to which religious forms of life involve metaphysical claims. Norman Malcolm and D.Z. Phillips have promoted this approach to religion. It may be considered *non-realist* in the sense that it does not treat religious beliefs as straightforward metaphysical claims that can be adjudicated philosophically as either true or false concerning an objective reality. By their lights, the

[6] *Ibid.*, p. 97.

traditional metaphysics of theism got what it deserved when it came under attack in the mid-twentieth century by positivists.

This Wittgensteinian challenge appears to place in check much of the way philosophers in the West have approached religion. But it has been charged that Wittgensteinian non-realism does not preserve but instead undermines the very intelligibility of religious practice.

Wittgenstein's influence in the philosophy of religion is due to scattered remarks, marginalia, and students' notes. He never intended to publish any material on the subject, and never wrote about it systematically. Nevertheless, it is possible to glean a moderately clear picture of his views about the nature and justification of religious beliefs. Yet his philosophy is permeated with a religious spirit. It was one of his strongest convictions that religion should be shown and demonstrated in everything rather than talked about as a separate matter. His reserve on the subject of religion arose not only from his feeling that it is more important to talk to God than to talk about God, but also from his awareness that in the present age religious expressions are almost certain to be misunderstood. (Thus he considered dedicating one of his books, later published after his death as *Philosophical Remarks,* "to the glory of God," but decided against it.) His semantic doctrine is an ingenious application of a powerful strategy, which consists in making “a radical break with the idea (which lay at the heart of the *Tractatus*) that language always functions in one way, always serves the same purpose: to convey thoughts which may be about houses, pains, good and evil, or anything else you please” (PI, 304). This strategy produced radical and fruitful ideas in the philosophy of mind and the philosophy of mathematics. Its application in the philosophy of religion has a kinship with both (but is less successful than either).

What is evident from the study of Wittgenstein’s life and work is that he was a clear cut “super naturalist”, in the sense that he sharply separated God from the world. Religion for Wittgenstein was a matter of belief, and such beliefs outranked any explanations, reasons, or logic. Wittgenstein had no patience with either sociological or psychological “explanations” of religion, and even less with scientific attempts to bolster religion or to create religious emotions as responses to scientific wonders. Religion had to do with a different and more important dimension than that of fact: the dimension of how we are to live.

Wittgenstein’s most important documents regarding religion are *Lectures and Conversations on Religious Belief* (Oxford, 1966) and *Remarks on Frazer’s “Golden Bough”* (London, 1979). However, some oblique references to religious beliefs are found in his earlier works also, i.e., *Notebooks* 1914-1916 and *Tractatus*. Although the early period is dominated by his ethics, much of what is said about ethics has been applied to religious beliefs with the help of a few references found there in terms of the notions of *mystical, transcendental, inexpressible,* viewing *sub-specie aeternitatis.* Besides, as we have seen, there is a significant shift in Wittgenstein's philosophy from the earlier to the later period. This raises the vital question whether this shift affected his views on religious beliefs or not. There are diverse opinions of thinkers regarding this. Some thinkers like Toulmin believe that Wittgenstein's earlier views on religious beliefs are not tenable in his later philosophy. On the other hand, some like Cyril Barrett believe that there is no radical change in his views so far as religious beliefs are concerned. And some like R. Rhees and D.Z. Phillips do not seem to be affected by the changes or are unaware of them. I find first standpoint as the most convincing. So, here in this work, I will confine myself to Wittgenstein's views on religious beliefs in the light of his theory of language games.

To recapitulate: In the 1930s, Wittgenstein's philosophy of language was dramatically transformed, and his earlier view of religion could not survive the transformation. He eventually came to believe that the picture of language he had pointed in the *Tractatus* was in error. Principally, he felt that all he had done was to describe one form of language — the language of science — and then to state dogmatically that all forms of language had to conform to this type or else be nonsensical. In his later work, the *Philosophical Investigations,* Wittgenstein attempts to overturn his earlier philosophy of language. He abandoned the doctrines that a proposition is a logical picture compounded out of names whose meanings are the things they stand for, and that the intelligible use of language always serves a single purpose i.e. to describe the facts. On the contrary, he came to believe that the meaning of a word is its use in the language; that words can be used for an indefinitely broad and heterogeneous range of purposes; and hence that the task of philosophy is not logical analysis but the description of our various "language-games". Since speech and writing are part and parcel of human activities in which it takes place and have significance only in the context of human forms of life and culture, the question of what an expression in a language means can only be answered by considering it in its context, and by asking how it is used. Thus, language has no general form; rather, it is a loose relation of varying linguistic practices. He argues that because of the way language looks when it is written down, or how it sounds when it is spoken, we tend automatically to think that it serves always the same function. This, says Wittgenstein, would be like thinking that all those things we call 'games' have the same purpose, or at least manifest some common element. He attempts to undermine this assumption:

> Instead of producing common to all that we call language, I am saying that these phenomena have no one thing in common which makes us use the same word for all, but that they are *related* to one another in many different ways. And it is because of this relationship, or these relationships, that we call them all 'language'. (PI, 65)

If we recognize that language may manifest itself in many varied forms – compare the language of poetry with the language of physics then we may no longer be tempted to proclaim that if language does not serve to express facts, then it is without sense.

We can see, then, that Wittgenstein's later account of language is less restrictive than the position he adopts in the *Tractatus.* There are in reality many spheres of discourse, just as there are many games, each with their own rules, each with their own standards of truth, falsity and meaning of course, one consequence of this is that if religious discourse does not conform to the standards of the scientific, then it is no longer to be confined to the realm of the unsayable. Just because the language of religion does not 'picture' empirical facts, we should not presume that it is without meaning.

For the later Wittgenstein, the meaning of a word or of a sentence is not always equated with the object or fact it represents. Language is no longer for him a static thing, whereby we describe states of affairs to each other. No, it is a dynamic practice, and the emphasis falls on the use of words, rather than what they represent. So: "for a large class of cases – though not for all – in which we employ the word "meaning" it can be defined thus: the meaning of a word is its use in the language. And the meaning of a name is sometimes explained by pointing to its bearer" (PI, 43). If we are puzzled by the meaning of certain expressions in a particular sphere of discourse we should not automatically consider what that expression *depicts*. Rather, we should look to see how it is *used*, what role it plays in that linguistic activity.

By virtue of these thoughts, when the later Wittgenstein writes about religious belief, he continues to argue that the use of language to express religious beliefs is quite unlike the use of language to state facts; but he no longer infers that it must therefore be a *misuse* of language. His principal aim is to explain how concepts such as sin, redemption, judgment, grace, and atonement can have an indispensable place in an individual's or a community's way of life, and to show how we can resist assimilating the use of these concepts to hypotheses, predictions, and theoretical explanations. In sum, he defends two principles;

First, a doctrine about the meaning of religious discourse which states that the expression of a religious belief in words is not a prediction or a hypothesis, but "something like a passionate commitment to a system of reference"; and, *Second*, a doctrine about the epistemology of religious beliefs which means religious belief is (equally) immune from falsification and from verification.

Critics and apologists who mistake religious beliefs for hypotheses and try to find evidence in their favours or against them confuse religious faith and superstition. Wittgenstein says, "Religious faith and superstition are quite different. One of them results from *fear* and is a sort of false science. The other is a trusting."[7]

Wittgenstein's response to Frazer's natural history of religion may help to clarify this. Frazer wants to say that religious practices are futile attempts to influence the course of nature, and that such rituals are the applications of an elementary and erroneous form of science. In other words, religion is false science. For Wittgenstein, this is a bizarre conclusion, produced by the illusion that all human action and belief must be akin to one paradigm: the scientific. Hence, he writes:

---

[7] Wittgenstein, Ludwig, *Culture and Value*, op. cit., p. 72.

> Frazer's account of the magical and religious notions of men is unsatisfactory: it makes these notions appear as mistakes. Was Augustine mistaken, then, when he called on God on every page of the Confessions?
>
> Well – one might say – if he was not mistaken, then the Buddhist holy-man, or some other, whose religion expresses quite different notions, surely was. But *none* of them was making a mistake except where he was putting forward a theory.[8]

The contention here is that it is only if we see religion as consisting of a set of theories, or hypotheses, about the nature of the world – that is, if we see religion as a species of science– that it begins to look mistaken. Wittgenstein is keen to stress that religion is precisely not theoretical in character. So belief in God is not to be equated with adherence to the hypothesis that somewhere or other there is a being called 'God'. To put it another way, believing in God is not akin to believing in the monster.

Wittgenstein shows the logical distinctiveness of religion and science in his 'Lectures on Religious Belief', where he considers the status, not of primitive beliefs and rituals, but of certain Christian doctrines. For example, he talks at length about the belief that there will be a Last Judgment. His stated

---

[8] Wittgenstein, Ludwig, *Remarks on Frazer's Golden Bough,* Doncaster: Brynmill Press, 1979, p. 1.

intention is to show that "in religious discourse we use such expressions as: 'I believe that so and so will happen', differently to the way in which we use them in science".[9] Here, he wants to know what is at stake between someone who does believe in such a judgment and someone who does not. So he considers two people, one of whom, whenever debating the course of action to take or whenever something bad happens to him, thinks of punishment. If he is ill, he thinks 'What have I done to deserve this?', if he is ashamed, he thinks 'This will be punished'. The other person (the unbeliever) just does not think of punishment at all. But this is no contradiction of the believer, for they are not disagreeing over whether a particular event will occur. However, he argues in favor of a far more radical doctrine, namely, that believing in the Last Judgment does not mean thinking it certain or probable that a certain kind of event will occur sometime in the future. This does not merely distance the use of an expression like, "I believe that so and so will happen" in religious discourse from its use in science, but from any kind of prediction at all.

So, if the expression "I believe that there will be a Last Judgment" is not used to make a prediction, how is it used? This is Wittgenstein's answer:

> Here believing obviously plays much more this role: suppose that a certain picture might play the role of constantly admonishing me, or

---

9 Wittgenstein, Ludwig, *Lectures and Conversations on Aesthetics, Psychology and Religious Belief*, ed. C. Barrett, Oxford! Blackwell, 1970, p. 57.

I always think of it. Here there would be an enormous difference between those people for whom the picture is constantly in the foreground, and others who just didn't use it at all.[10]

This example is not a typical one. Wittgenstein equates having religious belief with using religious concepts and having the attitudes and emotions that their use implies. He says this most explicitly as follows: "It strikes me that a religious belief could only be something like a passionate commitment to a system of reference. Hence, although it's belief, it's a way of living, or a way of assessing life. It's passionately seizing hold of this interpretation. Instruction in a religious faith, therefore, would have to take the form of a portrayal, a description, of that system of reference, while at the same time being an appeal to conscience.[11]

Wittgenstein says;

"Life can educate one to a belief in God. And *experiences* too are what bring this about; but I don't mean visions and other forms of sense experience which show us "the existence of this being", but, e.g. sufferings of various sorts. These neither show us God in the way a sense-impression shows us an object, nor do they give rise to

---

[10] *Ibid.*, p. 56.

[11] *Culture and Value*, op. cit., p. 64.

conjectures about him. Experiences, thoughts, life can force this concept on us."[12]

Here, Wittgenstein examines the role played by religious beliefs in the guidance of life and attempts to disentangle them from all factual matters, including claims about existence. He makes the important point that denying a religious belief or disagreeing with it is not contradicting anything, since the essence of religious belief has nothing to do with whether something is or is not the case, or was or will be the case. Rather, it has to do with how we live and die. When people are willing to suffer and die for their religious beliefs, it is not for some factual proposition that they are willing to suffer or die, though it may appear so. Thus, a belief in the Last Judgment should not be taken as an assertion that a certain event is or is not going to take place, but as something like an icon guiding our thoughts and actions, particularly in times of crisis. The attempt to make religious beliefs appear reasonable Wittgenstein regarded as often "ludicrous".

So, for Wittgenstein, belief in the Last Judgement is not a hypothesis, but rather a regulating or admonishing *picture*, in the same way that the 'all-seeing eye of God' might function as a picture which restrains us from immoral inclinations. This view of Wittgenstein has superficial similarity

---

[12] *Ibid.*, p. 86.

with that of Braithwaite's; but unlike him, Wittgenstein believes that religious beliefs are entirely non-reducible. To explain this, he considers someone saying to another, 'we might see one another after death'. A student in Wittgenstein's class responds by saying, 'in this case, you might only mean that he expressed an attitude'. But Wittgenstein rejects such a response and says, "No, it isn't the same as saying "I'm fond of you" and it may not be the same as saying anything else. It says what it says. Why should you be able to substitute anything else?'[13] For him, these religious pictures, far from being reducible to other statements (e.g. ethical ones), actually *constitute* a particular way of looking at the world. If they are not used, then that view of the world is ignored; and if a religion dies, then perspective dies with it.

For Wittgenstein, then, religion is not a speculative affair, and it is not the result of a cool contemplation of the world. It is, rather, grounded in a kind of instinctual reaction (which he calls a 'primitive reaction'). Out of such a reaction, a whole system of beliefs can develop. But these beliefs have no explanatory value and they are not theoretical. Such a character of religion is best captured in a remark from *Culture and Value*: "It strikes me that a religious belief could only be something like a passionate commitment to a

[13] Wittgenstein, *Lectures and Conversations on Aesthetics, Psychology and Religious Belief*, op. cit., p. 71.

system of reference. Hence, although it's *belief*, it's really a way of living, or a way of assessing life. It's passionately seizing hold of *this* interpretation".[14]

Through the notion of his analysis of the concept of language-game, he challenged the assertion that proof or evidence has anything to do with religious beliefs. According to him, the role of religion is important because it gives human kind an avenue from which essential existential and religious question can be addressed. The goal of the religious language-game is not to determine how the world operates, but rather to help solve the "riddles of life". (PI, 90)

He vehemently said that reasons, evidences and proofs have nothing to do with the formulation of religious belief which is neither rational nor irrational but something separate and distinct from the concept of rationality because rationality plays no role in the language-game of religion but of science. The language-game of science and religion is different from each other. He in his lecture says, "The depth grammar that regulates the religious language-game is different than the depth grammar that regulates science. He also postulates that as long as the primary goal of a particular language-game is different from another, they are immune to criticism from each other. Different religions have different language-games. Religious language-game is not an inclusive subset of any organized religion. Organized religions may

[14] Wittgenstein, L., *Culture and Value*, op. cit., p. 64.

serve as a vehicle for answering the questions of life. He wants true religious beliefs to be distinguished from superstition. Commenting on Father O' Hara's attempt to offer scientific arguments he remarks,

> "If this is religious belief, then it is superstition and he then says of O' Hara, here is a man who is cheating himself."[15]

Just as religious beliefs are misunderstood if conceived of as hypotheses, so rituals are misunderstood if they are thought to be attempts to manipulate the natural order. Wittgenstein rejects Frazer's view of the instrumental character of ritual by appealing to the numerous practical skills that members of primitive societies possess: "The same savage who, apparently in order to kill his enemy, sticks his knife through a picture of him, really does build his hut of wood and cuts his arrow with skill and not in effigy".[16] The force of Wittgenstein's point is this: Frazer maintains that the savage is so stupid that he cannot even conceive the distinction between the natural and the supernatural, so if he wants to kill his enemy, he kills him in effigy and does not retort to more practical means, like stabbing or poisoning him. Wittgenstein responds by saying that if this is the case, then these savages would surely hunt an effigy, build an effigy, marry an effigy, and so on. But they do not do this, and have, indeed, fairly sophisticated

---

15 *Lectures and Conversations on Aesthetics, psychology and Religious Belief*, op. cit., p.57.

16 Wittgenstein, Ludwig, *Remarks on Frazer's Golden Bough*, op. cit., p. 4.

agricultural and technical skills. So when a member of a primitive culture wants to plough a field, he does not simply imitate the action of ploughing.

This suggests to Wittgenstein that magic and religion are not of a kind with scientific, or practical, activities; they are not collections of errors, nor are they 'proto-science'. So what character do they have? Here is one suggestion:

> Burning in effigy or kissing the picture of a loved one. This is obviously not based on a belief that it will have a definite effect on the object which the picture represents. It aims at some satisfaction and it achieves it. Or rather, it does not aim at anything; we act in this way and then feel satisfied.[17]

Hence, just like the primitive age we perform rituals; we kiss pictures of people we love; we sometimes kiss their names; we mutilate pictures of those people we despise or who have hurt us. But we do not perform these actions in order to achieve any real concrete end (for example, the death of the person who has hurt us). Rather, these actions satisfy some of our emotional needs. For allied soldiers fighting in the Second World War, throwing darts at pictures of Hitler was not regarded as an easy or even possible method of assassination. Rather, such actions constituted an expression of their hatred for the enemy. Wittgenstein therefore writes:

[17] *Ibid.*, p. 8.

> When I am furious about something, I sometimes beat the ground or a tree with my walking stick. But I certainly do not believe that the ground is to blame or that my beating can help anything. "I am venting my anger'. And all rites are of this kind. Such actions may be called Instinct-actions.[18]

This suggests a very different picture of the nature of religious beliefs both from the account offered by Frazer and from the philosophical theism. Wittgenstein's view is that, far from being a theory concerning super-empirical entities or a metaphysical explanation, religion is an expression of human values, needs and desires.

Now, it was one of the fundamental themes of Wittgenstein's later philosophy that the concepts we use cannot be justified by reference to reality. Some philosophers have argued that our concepts, or at any rate the concepts of science, are correct, that they conform to the nature of the things we use them to describe. Wittgenstein argues that our network of concepts, which he calls *grammar*, cannot either conflict or accord with the facts. For what one says conflicts with the facts if it is false and accords with the facts if it is true. The concepts we use determine what it makes sense to say; and only what it makes sense to say is capable of being either true or false.

---

[18] Wittgenstein, Ludwig, 'Remarks on Frazer's Golden Bough', in C.G. Lockhart (ed.), *Wittgenstein: Sources and Perspectives*, Hassocks: Harvester, 1979, p. 72.

Grammar itself is therefore *arbitrary*, i.e. not accountable to any reality (This does not mean unimportant, capricious, or readily alterable). A system of measurement, for example, is not correct or incorrect in the way that a statement of length is; although of course some systems are more useful, convenient, and easy to take in and apply than others.

So, if Wittgenstein is right, religious beliefs are not *true* or *false;* and they are not *reasonable* or *unreasonable* either which means that they can, or cannot be justified:

> I would say, they are certainly not reasonable, that's obvious. "Unreasonable" implies, with everyone, rebuke. I want to say: they don't treat this as a matter of reasonability. Anyone who reads the Epistles will find it said: not only that it is not reasonable, but that it is folly. Not only is it not reasonable, but it doesn't pretend to be.[19]

The people Wittgenstein regards as *un*reasonable are apologists for, or against religion who make this assumption, Wittgenstein calls it "ludicrous". The religious beliefs can be corroborated or falsified by evidence. But unless religion is confused in this way with something quite different, it is not *un*reasonable. "Why shouldn't one form of life culminate in an utterance of

[19] Wittgenstein, Ludwig, *Lectures and Conversations on Aesthetics, Psychology and Religious Belief*, op. cit., p. 58.

belief in a Last Judgment?"[20] Wittgenstein asks rhetorically. And this immunity from rational criticism extends even to Christian beliefs about Jesus:

> The historical accounts in the Gospels might, historically speaking, be demonstrably false and yet belief would lose nothing by this... because historical proof (the historical proof-game) is irrelevant to belief.[21]

While concluding, I can say that according to Wittgenstein religious beliefs and belief in God is no longer subject to proof or evidence or empirical justification. The religious point of view is how one answers the existential question, or how one sees the world. This theory of religious beliefs is like the rest of Wittgenstein's language-game analysis. He is not denying science as today's society relies largely upon the theories and principles of science as much as he is preserving the rightful place of religion as an important part of life. We need religious point of view to tell us about our existence.

Wittgenstein says, "We feel that even when all possible scientific questions have been answered, the problems of life have still not been touched at all. Of course there is then no question left, and just this is the answer."[22]

* * *

---

[20] *Ibid.*, p. 57.

[21] Wittgenstein, Ludwig, *Culture and Value*, op. cit., p. 32.

[22] Ludwig Wittgenstein, *Tractatus Logico-Philosophicus*, trans. C.K. Ogden, Routledge, London, 1922, 6.52.

CHAPTER-V

WITTGENSTEIN'S AND ISLAMIC CONCEPT OF RELIGIOUS BELIEF

> Mohammad bhi tera, Jibreil bhi, Quran bhi tera
> Magar ye harf-e-sheereen tarjuman tera hai ya mera.
> (Mohammad is your's, Jibreil is your's, Quran is also your's
> But this sweet translated words are your's or mine.)
>
> – Mohd. Iqbal, *Bal-e-Jibreel*

> Perhaps one could 'convince someone of God's existence' through a certain kind of upbringing, by shaping his life in such and such a way.
>
> – Ludwig Wittgenstein, *Vermischte Bemerkungen*

I have divided this chapter into two schemes. In the first section, I have discussed the concept of religious beliefs according to Wittgenstein and Islam. In the second section, I have discussed the points of similarities between Islamic and Wittgenstein's concept of religious beliefs.

Section-I

According to Wittgenstein, religious beliefs do not purport to be statement of logical facts. The category of "truth, false or mechanical" which applies to statements of facts is not applicable to the statements expressing religious beliefs. In his book *On Certainty* he says that the grounds of very few of our beliefs have ever been tested. Its grounds are not in themselves either true or false or grounded. He says,

> "If the true is what is grounded, then the ground is not true, nor yet false."[1]

He further says that our religious beliefs are well-established, well-founded and properly grounded and these are not only accidental features but an essential feature of them. As he says,

> "But what men consider reasonable or unreasonable alters. At certain periods men find reasonable what at other periods they found unreasonable and vice-versa. But is there no objective character here? Very intelligent and well educated people believe in the story of creation in the Bible, while other hold it as proven false and the grounds of the latter are well known to the former."[2]

One of the remarkable points which Wittgenstein made around 1937 is the belief in the resurrection of the Christ. He says,

> "What inclines even me to believe in Christ's resurrection? It is as though I play with the thought. If he did not rise from the dead then he decomposed in the grave like any other man. He is dead and decomposed. In that case he is a teacher like any other and can no longer help. So we have to content ourselves with wisdom and speculation. But if I am to REALLY saved,-what I need is certainty,

---

1 *On Certainty*, op. cit., 205, p. 33.

2 *Ibid.*, 336, pp. 51-52.

> not wisdom, dreams or speculations-and this certainty is faith. And faith is what is needed by my heart, my soul but not by my speculative intelligence. For, it is my soul with its passions, as it were with its flesh and blood that has to be saved not my abstract mind. Perhaps we can say: only love can believe the resurrection."[3]

In one of the remarks made towards the end of his life in *Culture and Value,* he compared a religious believer with a tightrope walker. He says,

> "An honest religious thinker is like a tightrope walker. He almost looks as though he were walking on nothing but air. His support is the slenderest imaginable. And yet it really is possible to walk on it."[4]

In the above metaphor given by Wittgenstein it is not an intellectual support. It comes from love, trust and faith in the sense of trust meaning "having faith in".

Wittgenstein, after discussing the implicit nature of religious beliefs produces three elements that characterize religious belief:

(1) Its precariousness (on a tightrope, on the edge of an abyss) and yet managing to maintain its hold, its equilibrium,

---

3 *Culture and Value*, op. cit., p. 33.

4 *Ibid.*, p. 73.

(2) Its support : love, trust, belief and faith in the world of another; and

(3) Certainty, unshakable, steadfast faith.

Out of the three, Wittgenstein was interested in the last characteristic and says that religious belief is not based on intellectual certitude but on love and trust. And yet it is held with all the psychological certainty with which we hold the truth of mathematics. It is a firm, steadfast and unshakable belief. The underlying reason behind is that if we love someone enough to trust his word, this trust, this belief in his word is unshakable. Only distrust or weakening of trust can shake it. We are certain of the truth of the mathematical proposition because of their intrinsic logical structure. Religious believers are certain of their belief in spite of their having no intrinsic logical cohesion and very little extrinsic support.

Religious belief is a belief in God and as such is something more than the belief that God exists. Wittgenstein says,

> "Perhaps one could convince someone that God exists by means of a certain kind of upbringing by shaping his life in such and such a way. Life can educate one to a belief in God. And experiences too are what bring this about e.g. suffering of various sorts. These neither show us God in the way a sense impression shows us an object, nor do they give rise to conjectures about him. Experiences,

> thoughts- life can force this concept on us. So perhaps it is similar to the concept 'object'.[5]

Wittgenstein very categorically said that the existence of God cannot be proved. Any attempt to rationalize religious beliefs, dogma, theology, apologetic and such like will distort the language of religious beliefs. The religious point of view is how one answers the existential question, or how one sees the world.

As Wittgenstein says in *Culture and Value*:

> "God's essence is supposed to guarantee his existence-What this really means is that what is here at issue is not the existence of something. Could not one actually say equally well that the essence of colour guarantees its existence? As opposed, say, to white elephant. Because all that really means is: I cannot explain what 'colour' is, what the word "colour" means, except with the help of a colour sample. So in this case there is no such thing as explaining 'what it would be like if colour were to exist'."[6]

Now we might say: there can be a description of what it would be like if there were gods on Olympus-but not: what it would be like if there were

---

5 *Ibid.*, p. 86.

6 *Ibid.*, p. 82.

such a thing as 'God'. And to say this is to determine the concept 'God' more precisely. How are we taught the word 'God'? I cannot give a full grammatical description of it. But I can, as it were, make some contributions to such a description; I can say a good deal about it and perhaps in time assemble a sort of collection of examples."[7]

He further says,

> "The way you use the word 'God' does not show who you mean but rather, what you mean."[8]

He raised the question whether, in relation to religion, the non-believer contradicts the believer when he says that he does not believe what the believer believes. If one man contradicts another, they can be said to share a common understanding to be playing the same game. Consider the following example:

The man who says that the sun is 90 million miles away from the earth contradicts the man who says that the sun is only 20 million miles away from the earth. With the help of this example, what are we to say about the man who believes in God and the man who does not? Are they contradicting each other? Are two people, one of whom says there is a God

---

[7] *Ibid.*, p. 82.

[8] *Ibid.*, p. 52.

and the other of whom says he does not believe in God, like two people disagree about the distance of the sun from earth? Wittgenstein shows that they are not. The main reason for the difference is that God's reality is not one of a kind; He is not a being among beings. The word 'God' is not the name of a thing. Thus, the reality of God cannot be assessed by a common measure which also applies to things other than God. But these are conclusions for which reasons can be given.

In a reported conversation in Schlick's house on 17 December 1930, he asks: "Is talking essential to religion"? He replies:

> "I can well imagine a religion in which there are no doctrinal propositions in which thus there is no talking. Obviously the essence of religion cannot have anything to do with the fact that there is talking or rather: when people talk this itself is part of a religious act and not a theory".[9]

He was not concerned with the words or formulae we use but with the part they play in our religious life. Towards the end of his life, he put his views forcefully in some remarks. As he says,

> "It is true that we can compare a picture that is firmly rooted in us to a superstition; but it is equally true that we always eventually have

[9] C. Barrett, *Wittgenstein on Ethics and Religious Belief,* op. cit., p. 186.

> to reach some ground, either a picture or something else, so that a picture which is at the root of all our thinking is to be respected and not treated as a superstition. If Christianity is the truth then all the philosophy that is written about it is false."[10]

In his lecture and Conversation he said whether we believe and what we believe must be judged not by reasoning or ordinary grounds for belief but by how we regulate our lives in accordance with what we claim to believe.

He is not concerned with the claims about the existence of God, the creation of the world or the creation and the nature of human soul. What he objects to is Father O'Hara's claim, as he sees it, that Christianity rests on historical basis. He does not deny there is a historical basis for Christianity. What he says is that it does not afford sufficient evidence for Christian belief. Here we have a belief in historical facts different from a belief in ordinary historical facts. Even they are not treated as historical, empirical proposition. [11]

The content of the lectures on religious belief can be organised under three headings:

---

[10] *Culture and Value*, op. cit., p. 83.

[11] *Lectures and Conversations on Aesthetics, Psychology and Religious Belief*, op. cit., p. 57.

(1) The Logical Distinctiveness of Religious Belief:

Wittgenstein remarks upon the fact that we learn to speak in a religious way very early in life. The word 'God' is amongst the earliest learnt. Although this word is used like a word representing a person, he says, "If the question arises as to the existence of God it plays an entirely different role to that of the existence of any person or object I ever heard of."

(2) Religious Belief as 'Using Pictures':

Religious believers might say that a man is not really dead, even though by ordinary criteria he is. That is to say they think of him as really alive even though he is what we all call dead. They speak of him as a disembodied spirit. What Wittgenstein wants to know is whether or not one can connect with these words. There is a 'technique of usage' for the word dead considered as 'a public instrument'. He suggests that pictures of God are not used like pictures of aunts. No one presents you with a picture of God.

(3) The Essential Difference between Believers and Unbelievers:

According to Wittgenstein, believers use the relevant pictures with the relevant connections; non-believers do not. Using a picture, if it is to serve as a definition of religious belief cannot, however, be simply a matter of accepting, or rejecting, logical implication of propositions such as 'God's eye sees everything'. Considering all of this, it is surely right to say that Wittgenstein's mature life was strongly marked by religious thought and feeling. He was more deeply religious than are many people who correctly regard themselves as religious believers. Wittgenstein had an intense desire for moral and spiritual purity. Of course I want to be perfect; he exclaimed. He judged himself to be neither a creative philosopher nor a religious person. But I can say with confidence that he knew the demands of religion. And certainly he was as qualified as any philosopher ever had been to understand what it might mean to see the problem of philosophy from a religious point of view.

Regarding the religious belief in Islam, *Allah* says in chapter two of *The Quran:*

> "O ye who believe; believe in God and His apostle and the scriptures which He has send to his apostle and the scriptures which He sent to those before. Anyone who denies God, His angels, His books, His apostle and the day of Judgement has gone far, far astray." (4:136)

If your belief is by habit or birth the example of those you love or respect or admire make that belief more specific and special to yourself. We must not only have faith but realise that faith in our innermost being. The chief objects of our faith are God, His apostle, His revelations. To all these we must give a home in our hearts. The angels we do not see and realise as we realise God, who is nearer to us than the vehicle of our life blood, and the day of Judgement is for our future experience but we must not deny them or we cut off a part of our spiritual view.

The Islamic philosophy and religion is based upon the belief that *Allah* transmitted knowledge to Prophet Mohammad and other Prophets in the form of *The Quran* which is the formless word of God. *The Quran* is the sacred book of Islam which was revealed to the Prophet Mohammad by the angel Gabreil on various occasions from 610-632 B.C.

The Prophet from time to time had seen visions but his first experience of higher revelation was when he was alone in the cave of *Hira.* It is clearly mentioned in one of *Hadith* of the Prophet:

> "He (Gabriel) squeezed me and he squeezed me to such an extent that I was quite exhausted and this was repeated thrice."[12]

There are verses in *The Quran* which show that the collection of the book was a part of the Divine scheme. These verses:

---

12 *Al-Bukhari,* op. cit., 1:1.

"Surely on us rests the collecting of it and the reciting of it." (75:17)

Though *The Quran* was revealed in portions yet it is a mistake to suppose that it remained for long in those fragmentary conditions. *The Quran* itself is clear on this point:

> "And those who reject our faith and say: why *The Quran* was not revealed to him all at once?" (25:32)

Three reasons are given in *The Quran* itself for its gradual revelation,

(1) To strengthen thy heart.

(2) Slow, well-arranged stages.

(3) Questions put and answers given.

The basis of Muslim belief is Kalma (*shahadah): La ilaha-illallahu; Muhammadur-rasulu-llahi*, meaning, "There is no God but *Allah* and Prophet Muhammad is the messenger of *Allah*." To have full faith in this statement is indispensible for a person to become Muslim. This statement is further included in the five pillars of Islam. The five pillars are as follows:

(1) Kalma (*Shahadah*): It is a saying professing monotheism and accepting Muhammad as the messenger of *Allah*. When a person wishes to convert he should recite this affirmation and believe in it.

(2) Daily prayer (*Salah*): It is a daily prayer of Islam. It consists of five-time prayers.

(3) Charity (*Zakat*): It is the obligatory charity given by every Muslims to the poor which is 2.5% of their income. It is considered to be a personal responsibility for Muslims to ease economic hardship for others and eliminate inequality. The word *Zakat* means purification. Our wealth is purified by giving a proportion to those in need and to society in general. Like the pruning of plants, this cutting back balances and encourages new growth.

(4) *Sawm* (Fasting): Muslims observe fast every year during the month of Ramadan from dawn to dusk which is abstaining from drinking, eating and sexual relation with their spouse. It is not obligatory on those who are sick, elderly or on journey, women who are menstruating, pregnant and nursing. They make up an equal number of days later in the year if they are healthy and able. It is a method of self-purification and self-restraint. As *Allah* says in *The Quran:*

> "O you who believe, Fasting is prescribed for you as it was prescribed to those before you that you may learn self-restraints." (2:183)

(5) *Hajj* (Pilgrimage): It is an obligation to those who are physically and financially able to do so. Every year more than two million people go to *'Makkah'* from all over the world to perform *Hajj.* They wear simple garment that strip away distinctions of caste, class and culture so that all stand equal before *Allah.*

Section-II

In this section, I will discuss the points of similarities between Wittgenstein's and Islamic concept of religious beliefs. Some of the similarities between the two are as follows:

(1) In one conversation Wittgenstein made these remarks:

"Remember that Christianity is not a matter of saying a lot of prayer; in fact we are told not to do so. If you and I are to live a religious life it must not be that we talk a lot about religion but that our manner of life is different. It is my belief that only if you try to be helpful to other people you will in the end find your way to God."[13] What is being said is not that worship and praise have no place in a religious life, but rather than that they are worthless if there is no amending one's ways and one's doings. Like many other beliefs, religious beliefs too are matters of heart and soul, love,

---

13 Norman Malcolm, *Wittgenstein: A Religious point of View*? op. cit. P.11.

trust and faith. Wittgenstein had an intense desire for moral and spiritual purity. The similar viewpoint is given by the most important contemporary Islamic philosopher, Mohammad Iqbal in the third part of his famous collection of Ghazal *"Bang-e-Dara"* which was published in 1924. One of his famous couplets from this collection reveals his viewpoint about this:

> *"Jo main sar ba sajda hua kabhi to zamin se aane lagi sada*
> *Tera dil to hai sanam aashna tujhe kya milega namaz se."*[14]

The essence of this verse is that if your heart is not pure then there is no meaning in offering *namaz*. He says that when I did *Sajda* (one posture in *namaz*) then divine voice came and said that your heart is involved in materialistic world, your heart is *sanam aashna* (lover of worldly object), you will not get anything out of such type of prayer. Mohd Iqbal's main contention is that in religious activities dualism will not work. If you are not pure by heart, your intention is not pure, then your prayer is not accepted in the sight of *Allah*.

(2) In *Culture and Value,* Wittgenstein very clearly says that religion is a matter of faith or belief. In religion, God and faith are treated as the culminating point of explanations. That is where explanations come to an end. Explanations are internal to a language-game. Outside the

[14] Mohd. Iqbal, *Kulyat-e-Iqbal*, Educational Publishing House, Delhi, 2005, P. 281.

language-game or forms of life there are no explanations. The same concept that religion is a matter of faith or belief is repeated in *The Quran* and authentic *Hadith* of the Prophet which has already been discussed in chapter two of my thesis.

(3) Wittgenstein told his friend Drury, "If you and I are to live a religious life it must not be that we talk a lot about religion but that our manner of life is different." He added,

> "It is my belief that only if you try to be helpful to other people, you will in the end find your way to God."[15]

What he meant by this was not that all talk about religious practices, methods of worship has no place in religious life, rather what he meant was that all such talk is nonsense if there is no amending to one's ways and doings, or one's behaviour, in short one's mindset. It is our practice which determines whether we are religious or not.[16] The same concept is used in Islam where the primary importance is given on the conduct (*Ekhlaq*) of a person. It is said that religion does not mean talking a lot about religion but religion consist in doing. Wittgenstein says that if you try to be helpful to others you will in the

---

[15] Rush, Rhees (ed.), *Ludwig Wittgenstein: Personal Recollection,* Oxford: Basil Blackwell, 1981, p. 129.

[16] Vohra, Ashok, *JICPR,* Vol. XXIV, P. 74.

end find your way to God. The same concept is repeated in *The Quran* where *Allah* says:

> "By the token of time man is verily in a state of loss except those who have faith, righteous deeds, those who exhort people to truth and those who exhort people to patience and constancy." (103:1-3)

This sura clearly says that the faith is the armour which wards off the wounds of the material world and his righteous life is his positive contribution to the spiritual ascent. If a person lives only for himself he has not fulfilled his whole duty. Whatever good he has, especially in the moral and spiritual life, he must spread among his brethren, so that they may see the truth and stand by it in patient hope and unshakable constancy amidst all the storm and stress of outer life.

(4) According to Wittgenstein, religious belief is an absolute trust either in a book, in a being, in a Prophet, in a holy man, in a principle, in a doctrine, or all of them. Wittgenstein, by analyzing the concept of believing, says, "Believing means, submitting to an authority. Having once submitted to it, you cannot then, without rebelling against it, first call it in question and then once again find it convincing."[17] The

[17] *Culture and Value*, op. cit., p. 52.

same concept is repeated in *The Quran* and authentic *Hadith* of Prophet. Regarding faith, *Allah* says in *The Quran*:

> "O ye who believes, Believe in God and His apostle, and the scriptures which he has sent to his apostle and the scriptures which he has sent to those before Him. Anyone who denies God, His angels, His books, His apostle and the Day of Judgment, has gone far, far astray." (4:136)

Allah further says in *The Quran*:

> "It is not righteousness that ye turn your faces towards East or West; but it is righteousness to believe in *Allah,* the last day, the angels, the books and the Prophets." (2:177)

(5) According to Wittgenstein, religious belief is for the most part 'a priori' and based on faith and revelation and in it nothing can be proved. The same concept is repeated at so many places in *The Quran.* Examples of miracles in *The Quran* are the best examples of what does not depend on experience and based on faith. One example of this miracle is that *The Quran* was revealed to a person who was illiterate and this revelation was completed in parts in more than twenty two years time.

(6) According to Wittgenstein, religious belief is an unshakable commitment which guides a person's entire life which is well-

established, well-founded and properly grounded. He continues and says that religious belief is a way of life. The same concept is repeated in *The Quran* where it is repeated again and again that religious belief guides our entire life and not only the life after death. Religious belief is ethical as well as spiritual principle which guides our life in this world as well as the life after death, which is permanent life. As *Allah* says in *The Quran:*

> "Certainly we have created man in the best then we render him the lowest of the low except those who believe and do good, so there is a reward never to be cut off." (95:4-6)

(7) In 1948, towards the end of his life, Wittgenstein took the analogy of the tightrope walker and said,

> "An honest religious thinker is like a tightrope walker. He almost looks as though he were walking on nothing but air. His support is the slenderest imaginable. And yet it really is possible to walk on it."[18]

He further continues that religious belief is a belief in God and as such is something more than the belief that God exists. The same concept is repeated in Islam where it is said that a person who is an honest religious believer will never do any wrong. He will follow

[18] Cyril Barrett, *Wittgenstein on Ethics and Religious Belief,* op. cit., p. 182.

whatever is said in *The Quran* and authentic *Hadith* of Prophet Mohammad. If he does not do so then he is not an honest religious believer. In Islam also, religious belief means that only having faith or belief in God is not sufficient but you have to follow some basic rituals which is *'Fard'* in Islam i.e. *Kalma, Namaz, Saum, Zakat* and *Hajj*. If a person is not honest in following his *'Fard'* duties, he is not a true Muslim.

(8) Being a devout Christian, Wittgenstein accepted the monotheistic view of God. According to him, God is one who exists in three distinct forms i.e. Father, Son and Holy Spirit which is called 'the trinity' in Christianity. God, in Christianity is recognised as the real creator of this world. The relation between God and the creator is that of master and servant. The concept of God is similar in Islam where it is said, God is one who is not a trinity. The Islamic concept of God is called strict Monotheism. God, in Islam is also recognised as the real creator of this Universe. Regarding the relation between God and His creator it is said that:

> "We are nearer to him than his life-vein." (50:16)

It is further said:

> "We are nearer to it (the soul) than you." (56:85)

The idea that God is nearer to man than his own self only shows that the consciousness of the existence of God in the human soul is even clearer than the consciousness of its own existence.

(9) In his lecture on religious belief Wittgenstein threw these ideas together. "He supposed a person who believes in the Last Judgement and makes this his guidance for life. 'Whenever he does anything this is before his mind.' How are we to know whether this person believes in what he is saying, Wittgenstein asks. 'He has what you might call unshakable faith'."[19] Those who believe in Jesus Christ and submit their lives to his lordship will enjoy eternal bliss in heaven, where there will be no sorrow or pain, no disease or death. The belief in Last Judgement in Islam is the last ground of religious belief. According to *The Quran,* death is not the end of a man's life. It only opens the door to another, a higher form of life. As *Allah* says in *The Quran*:

> "We have ordained death among you and we are not to be overcome, that we have changed your state and make you grow into what you know not." (56:60)

[19] *Ibid.*, p. 179.

The life after death in Islam takes two forms; in the first is a life in paradise for those in whom the good exceeds the evil, and in the second is a life in Hell for those in whom the evil exceeds the good.

(11) According to Wittgenstein, miracles are not evidence for religious belief. They are certainly not sufficient evidence, as is popularly thought. He, therefore, concludes that neither the so-called proof for the existence of God are sufficient as a grounding of faith, nor are they other argument or alleged evidence. The believers have reasons for their belief. For him they are overwhelming reasons. But they do not amount to anything remotely resembling scientific evidence. An essential feature of religious belief is that it is not grounded in rational argument. The same concept is repeated in Islamic philosophy where it is said that no proof or any rational argument can be given for miracles. The existence of God cannot be proved by any rational argument. It is only a matter of faith.

* * *

CHAPTER-VI

A SCIENTIFIC STUDY OF ISLAM

> Khol aankh, zameen dekh, falak dekh, faza dekh
> Mashrik se ubharte hue suraj ko zara dekh.
> (Open your eyes, look at the earth, look at the sky, look at the environment
> Look at the sun which rises from the east.)
>
> – Mohd. Iqbal, *Bal-e-Jibreel*

> Philosophy is not one of the natural sciences.
>
> – Ludwig Wittgenstein, *Tractatus*

The misconception prevalent in the West that Islam is an unprogressive and static religion, antagonistic to science and civilization is totally baseless. But the fact is that it was only Islam which gave birth to modern science, started a scientific era in the world's history and made the early Muslims precursors of modern scientists and pioneers of modern civilization. However, the subsequent intellectual stagnation that over-shadowed the Muslim world was due to certain historical events similar to those that prevailed in Europe during the Middle Ages before the Renaissance and the Reformation. For this social degeneration and political debate the Islamic faith and its teaching were in no way responsible.

The Quran which is the main source of Islamic faith is considered by Muslims of Divine origin. Its preachings are directives and guidance for the whole of humanity. The teachings of *The Quran* are believed to be for all times and are relevant to every age. It is widely accepted that *The Quran* is the best Arabic literature on the face of the earth. To establish its superiority *The Quran* puts a challenge in the following verse:

> "And if you are in doubt as to what we have revealed from time to time to our servant, then produce a Surah like there unto; and call your witnesses or helpers besides *Allah* if you are true." (2:23)

Today's rational man would not accept religious scriptures which are not based on logic, reason and science. Many would not accept *The Quran's* extraordinarily beautiful language as proof of its Divine origin. Any scripture claiming to be a divine revelation must also be acceptable on the strength of its own reason and logic. The famous scientist Albert Einstein once said:

> "Science without religion is lame and religion without science is blind."

Let me therefore study *The Quran*, the most authentic source of Islam as a religion, in the light of modern science. *The Quran* contains more than 6600 verses out of which more than 1000 verses talk only about science. In what follows, I will discuss some aspects of science with reference to *The Quran*.

A) Creation of Heaven and Earth:

When we refer to the translations of *The Quran* we find that the creation took place over a period of six days. As *Allah* says in *The Quran:*

> "Your Lord is God who created the heaven and the earth in six days." (7:54)

The word 'days' here means not the ordinary days of twenty-four hours duration but 'long length of time', an indefinite period of time. The Arabic word used for this long length of time is *'Yaum',* which is further mentioned at so many places in *The Quran.* For example:

> "He rules all the affairs from the heaven to the earth which in the end will go up to him on a day, the space whereof will be a thousands years of your reckoning." (32:5)

The word *'Yaum'* is quite different from the period that we mean by the word 'day' struck very early commentators. These commentators did not have the knowledge we possess today concerning the length of the stages in the formation of the universe. Modern commentators have gone back to this interpretation. Abdullah Yusuf Ali in his commentary on each of the verses that deals with the stages in the creation insists on the importance of taking the word, elsewhere interpreted as meaning days, to mean in reality 'very long periods' or 'Ages'. It is obvious from the verses of *The Quran* that regarding the creation of the world it speaks for long periods of time numbering six. The longest passages in *The Quran* which deal with the creation of the universe are the following (*Allah* speaks to the Prophet).

"Say: Do you disbelieve who created the earth in two periods? Do you ascribe equal to Him. He is the Lord of the worlds.

He set in the earth mountain standing firm. He blessed it. He measured therein its sustenance in four periods in due proportion, in accordance with the needs of those who ask for sustenance.

Moreover He turned to heaven when it was smoke and said to it and to the earth: come willingly or unwillingly! They said: we come in willing obedience.

Then He ordained them seven heavens in two periods and He assigned to each heaven its mandate by revelation. And we adorned the lower heaven with luminaries and provided it a guard. Such is the decree of the All Mighty, the full of knowledge." (41:9-12)

The following verses of *The Quran* elucidate the phenomena that constitute the basic process of the formation of the universe. According to physicists, the creation of the Universe is explained by a widely accepted phenomenon popularly known as the 'Big Bang', which is supported by observational and experimental data gathered by astronomers and astrophysicists. The whole universe was initially one Primary Nebula (Big Mass). Then there was a secondary separation (Big Bang) which resulted in the formation of Galaxies. It further divided into stars, planets, the sun, and the moon etc. The following verse of *The Quran* mentions the origin of the universe:

> "Do not the unbelievers see that the heavens and the earth were joined together before we clove them asunder?" (21:30)

Scientists say that the celestial matter was initially in the form of gaseous matter before the formation of the galaxies. It means before the formation of the galaxies huge gaseous matter (clouds) were present. The word 'smoke' is more appropriate than 'gas' to describe initial celestial matter. *The Quran* mentions the word *'dukhan'* for smoke in the following verse:

> "Moreover, He comprehended in His design the sky and it had been as smoke. He said to it and to the earth 'come ye together, willingly or unwillingly'. They said we do come in willing obedience." (41:11)

2) Astronomy in *The Quran:*

Apart from the verses that specifically describe the creation there are roughly forty other verses in *The Quran* which provide information on astronomy. The general reflections concerning the sky are mentioned in the following verses of *The Quran*:

> "Do they not look at the sky above them how we have built it and adorned it and there is no rift in it." (50:6)

The greatest philosophers have found it difficult to understand the skeptical position when they contemplate the wonder and mystery of the skies with all the countless beautiful stars and planets and lights in them and laws of order, motion and symmetry that respond to the highest mathematical abstraction without a flaw.

The Quran further comments on this in the following verse:

> "God is the one who raised the heavens without any pillars that you can see them, he firmly established Himself on the throne. He has subjected the sun and the moon each one runs for a appointed term. He regulates all the affairs explaining the signs in detail that you may believe with certainty in the meeting with your Lord." (13:2)

We must not think that everything came into being by itself or carries out its function by itself. God is the active force through which everything has its life and being and through which everything is maintained and supported even though fixed laws are established for its regulation and governance. The term 'appointed' limits the duration of their functioning because its ultimate return is to God as its beginning proceeds from God. Where the laws of nature are fixed and everything runs according to its appointed course the governance and regulation behind it is still that of God, who cares for his creatures.[1]

One manifestation of his caring for His creatures even where a limited amount of free-will is granted for their development is that he is careful to explain His signs and detailed revelation through His messengers lest man should have any doubt whether he has to return ultimately to his Lord and account for all his actions during the 'term appointed.'

Earlier civilization believed that the moon emanates its own light but with the help of scientific discoveries now it is proved that the light of the moon is not its own light but the reflected light of the sun. The Arabic word, used in *The Quran* for sun is *'shams'*. It is referred to as *'Siraaj'* which means a torch or as *'wahaaj'* which further means a blazing lamp

1 *The Quran,* trans. A.Y. Ali, op. cit., ref. no. 1801, p. 602.

(shining glory). All the three descriptions are appropriate to the sun since it generates intense heat and light by its internal combustion. The Arabic word used in *The Quran* for moon is *'qamar'* and it is described in *The Quran* as *'Muneer'* which is a body that gives *'nur'* i.e. light.

Most of the science texts have mentioned the fact that the sun rotates about its axis and takes approximately twenty five days to complete one rotation. The sun travels through space at roughly 150 miles per second and takes about 200 million years to complete one revolution around the centre of our Milky Way galaxy. As it is mentioned in *The Quran*:

"It is not permitted to the sun to catch up the *'Nur'* nor can the night outstrip the day. Each swims along its own orbit according to law."(51:47)

This verse of *The Quran* mentions a very important fact proved by modern science, i.e. the existence of the individual orbits of the sun and the moon and their journey through space with their own motion.

We know that the stars are heavenly bodies which produce their own light. They are the scenes of various physical phenomena of which the easiest to observe is their generation of light. The term 'Star' comes from the root word *'Najm'*. The word designates a visible heavenly body without saying of what kind, i.e. either generator of light or mere reflector of light received. To make it clear that the object so designated is a star. The following verse of *The Quran* contains the qualifying phrase:

> "By the sky and the night-visitor who will tell thee what the night visitor is the star of piercing brightness." (86:1-3)

The star of piercing brightness is understood by some to be the morning star by others to be the planet Saturn, by still others to be *'Sirius'* or the shooting stars. The best way is to take the 'star' in the collective or generic sense for star shines on every night in the year and their piercing brightness is most noticeable on the darkest night.

The planets do not have their own light. They revolve around the sun. Five planets other than Earth were known to the ancients viz; Mercury, Venus, Mars, Jupiter and Saturn. Three have been discovered in recent times viz; Uranus, Neptune and Plato. *The Quran* mentions it by the name *Kankab* (plural *Kawakib*) without stating their numbers. The following verse of *The Quran* mentions it:

> "God is the light of the heavens and the earth. The similitude of His light is as if there were a niche and within it a luminary. The luminary is in a glass. The glass is as if it were a planet glittering like a pearl." (24:35)

Here the subject is the projection of light onto a body that reflects it and gives it the glitter of a pearl, like a planet that is lit by the sun. This is the only explanatory detail referring to it to be found in *The Quran.*

In 1925, Edwin Hubble proved that all galaxies are receding from one another which imply that the universe is expanding. The expansion of the universe is now an established scientific fact. This is what exactly *The Quran* says regarding the nature of the universe:

> "The heaven we have built it with power. Verily, we are expanding it." (51:47)

The Arabic word used in this verse is *'Musiun'* which means 'expanding it' which refers to the creation of the expanding vastness of the universe. In his book Stephen Hawking said that the discovery that the universe is expanding was one of the greatest intellectual revolution of the 20th century.

3) The Earth:

The discussion of the earth in the light of *The Quran* will be discussed under three broad headings:

(a) The water cycle and the seas,

(b) The Earth's relief,

(c) The Earth's atmosphere.

(a) The water cycle and the seas: In the seventh-century, Thales held the theory whereby the waters of the ocean under the effect of winds were thrust towards the interior of the continents so the water fell upon the earth and penetrated into the soil. Plato shared these views and thought that the return of the waters to the oceans was via great alloys. This theory had many supporters until the eighteenth-century, one of whom was Descartes. Aristotle imagined that the water vapour from the soil condensed in cool mountain caverns and formed underground lakes that fed springs. The first clear formulation of the water cycle must be attributed to Bernard Palissy in 1580. He claimed that underground water came from rainwater infiltrating into the soil.

The following verses of *The Quran* contain no trace of mistaken ideas that were current at the time of Prophet. As *Allah* mentions in *The Quran:*

> "We sent down from the sky blessed water whereby we caused to grow gardens, grains for harvest, tall palm trees with their spates piled one above the other sustenance for servants. Therewith we gave life to a dead land. So will be the emergence." (50:9-11)
>
> It is further said:
>
> "We sent down water from the sky in measure and lodged it in the ground. And we certainly are able to withdraw it. Therewith for you

we gave rise to gardens of palm-trees and vineyards where for you are abundant fruit and of them you eat." (23:18-19)

Normally the rain comes well distributed and soaks into the soil. The moisture is retained for a long time in all high grounds, it soaks and penetrates through many layers of soil and forms the architecture of physical geography. The retentive powers of higher soil enable the rivers to flow perennially even where the rainfall is seasonal and confined to a few months in the year. Another form in which water comes down from the sky according to due measure is in snow and hail which also have their place in the economy of air and soil. The verse also mentions about olive oil which is an ingredient in medicinal ointment and in ointment used for religious ceremonies such as the consecrations of kings. It, thus, has a symbolic meaning. If it is used for food, olive has a delicious flavour.

The following verses of *The Quran* mentions the water cycle in a very clear manner:

> "God is the one who sends forth the winds which rose up the clouds. We drive them to the dead land. Therewith we revive the ground after its death. So will be the resurrection." (35:9)

> "God is the one who sends forth the winds like heralds of His mercy. We cause pure water to descend in order to revive a dead

land with it and to supply with drink the multitude of cattle and human beings we have created." (48:49)

The Quran further Quotes:

"God sends water down from the sky so that the river flows according to their measure. The torrent bears away the foam that mounts up to the surface." (13:17)

Man cannot willfully break the established cycle that maintains the circulation of water in nature. When one compares the modern data on hydrology to what is contained in the numerous verses of *The Quran,* one has to admit that there is a remarkable degree of agreement between them.

A certain number of verses of *The Quran* deal with the seas and navigation. As subject for reflection they provide indication of divine omnipotence that arises from the facts of common observation. The following verses are examples of this:

"God has made the ship subject to you so that it runs upon the sea at His command." (14:32)

The Quran further explained:

"God is the one who subjected the sea, so that you eat fresh meat from it and you extract from it ornaments which you wear. Thou seest the ships plowing the waves, so that you seek of His bounty. May be you will be thankful." (16:14)

This verse of *The Quran* refers that we have gone up in a climax of material things from the big to the subtle in the sky and the earth. Here, we have another climax as regards the things of the sea. We get the delicate flesh of fishes and marine creatures of all kinds; get the treasure of the deep i.e. pearls, coral, amber and the things of that kind. Diving for pearl in both the primitive and the more advanced form is another instance of man's power over apparently inaccessible depths of the sea. After the material benefits which we get from the sea we are asked to consider things of higher import to the spirit of man. There is the beautiful ship which stands as the symbol of international commerce and interaction. These are the first steps in seeking of the bounty, 'bounty of God' through the sea. But this has some higher aspects. Navigation and international interaction increase knowledge which in its higher aspects should clean the mind and make it fitter to approach God. The salt water which covers nearly seventy two percent of the surfaces is itself a purifying and salinity agent and is a good symbol of the higher bounties of God which are as boundless as the ocean.

Modern science has discovered that in the places where two different seas meet, there is a barrier between them. This barrier divides the two seas so that each sea has its own temperature, salinity and density. Oceanologists are now in a better position to explain the verse of *The Quran* covering this. There is a slanted unseen water barrier between the two seas through which water from one sea passes to the other. But when the water from one sea enters the other sea it loses it distinctive characteristic and becomes homogenized with the other. In a way this barrier serves as a transitional homogenizing area for the two waters. Regarding this *Allah* mentions in *The Quran*:

> "He has loosed the two seas. They meet together. Between them there is a barrier which they do not transgress. Out of them come pearls and coral." (55:19-22)

It is further said in *The Quran:*

> "The two seas are not alike. The water of one is agreeable, sweet pleasant to drink and the other, salty and bitter. You eat fresh meat from it and you extract from it ornament which you wear." (35:12)

In addition to the description of the main fact, these verses refer to what may be obtained from fresh water and sea water.

B) The Earth's Relief:

The constitution of the Earth is highly complex. The history of the distribution of the sea and land on the surface of the globe has only recently been established and is still incomplete even for the most recent and best known periods. According to modern ideas, the dominating factors in the formation of the land that emerged were the development of mountain ranges.

When referring to the Earth's relief, *The Quran* only describes, as it were, the formation of the mountains. Seen from the present point of view, there is indeed little one can say about the verses that only express God's Beneficence to man with regard to the earth's formation, as *Allah* says in the following verses:

> "For you *Allah* made the earth a carpet so that you travel along its roads and the paths of valleys." (71:19-20)

As *Allah* further says in *The Quran*:

> "The earth, we have spread it out. How excellently we did that." (51:48)

The carpet which has been spread out is the earth's crust, a solidified shell on which we can live since the globe's sub-strata are very hot, fluid and hostile to any form of life. The statement in *The Quran* referring to the mountain and the references to their stability subsequent to the phenomenon of the folds are very important.

The following verses give details about the way in which the mountains were anchored in the ground:

> "Have we not made the earth an expanse and the mountains stakes." (78:6-7)

The spacious expanse of the earth may be compared to a carpet to which the mountains may metaphorically be supposed to act as pegs. The stakes referred to be the ones used to anchor a text in the ground. Modern geologists describe the fold in the earth as giving foundations to the mountains and their dimensions go roughly one mile to ten miles. The stability of the earth's crust results from the phenomenon of these folds.

The following verses express the idea that the way the mountains are laid out ensures stability and is in complete agreement with geological data:

> "And the mountains (*Allah*) have fixed them firmly." (79:32).
>
> "(*Allah*) has cast into the ground (mountains) standing firm so that it does not shake with you." (31:10).

C) The Earth's Atmosphere:

The Quran contains several passages dealing with the phenomena that occur in the atmosphere. So far as the comparison between them and the data of modern science is concerned it is to be noted that there is no contradiction between today's modern scientific knowledge and the phenomena described in *The Quran* mentions that a familiar feeling of discomfort experienced at high altitude which increases the higher one climbs. As it is expressed in *The Quran*:

> "Those whom God wills to guide, He opens their breast to Islam. Those whom He wills lose their way, He makes their breast narrow and constricted, as if they were climbing in the sky." (6:125)

The Quran also mentions the presence of electricity in the atmosphere and the consequence of this i.e. lightening and hail. As *The Quran* mentions this in the following two verses:

> "(God) is the one who shows you the lightening with fear and covetousness. He rose up the heavy clouds. The thunder glorifies his praise and so do the angels for awe. He sends the thunder-bolt and strikes with them whom He wills while they are disputing about God. He is Almighty in His power". (13:12-13)

> "Have you not seen that God makes the clouds move gently then joins them together then makes them a heap? And you see raindrops issuing from within it. He sends down from the sky mountains of hail. He strikes therewith whom He wills and He turns it away from whom He wills. The flashing of its lightening almost snatches away the sight." (24:43)

The phenomenon of shadows and the fact that they move is very simply explained today. As *The Quran* says:

> "It is Allah who made out of the things, He created something to give you shade..." (16:81)

This verse means the trees, gardens, and the roof of the houses gives you shade. From a different point of view it may be said that the fact that the sun's rays at various times and in various parts of the earth come obliquely causes shadows along with sunshine.

The Quran further speaks about it in the following verse:

> "Have (the unbelievers) not observed that for all the things God created how their shadow shifts right and left, prostrating themselves to God while they are full of humility." (16:48)

Here the word 'things' means inanimate things. By a metaphor even such inanimate things are spoken of as recognizing God and humbly worshiping Him. Even their shadows turnaround from right to left according to the light from the above. The 'shadows' suggest how all things in this life are mere shadows of the true reality in heaven and they should turn and move in accordance with the divine light as the shadows of the trees and buildings move in one direction or another and lengthen or shorten according to the light from the heaven.

4) The Animal and Vegetable Kingdom:

The Quran contains several references concerning the animal kingdom which are the subject of commands that call for a confrontation with modern scientific knowledge. As *The Quran* mentions:

> "Allah created cattle for you and you find in warmth, useful services and food, sense of beauty when you bring them home and when you take them to pasture. They bear your heavy load to lands you could not reach except with great personal effort. Verily your lord is compassionate and merciful. He created horses, mules and donkeys for you to ride and for ornament. And He created what you do not know." (16:5-8)

This verse of *The Quran* refers to so many things. It says that camel's hair makes warm robes and blanket and certain kinds of goats yields hair which makes similar fabrics. The females of many of these animals yield good warm milk which is nourishing and wholesome diet. The flesh of many of these animals is good to eat. The cattle and animals also carry loads and thus make inter-communication between different lands easy.

The Quran also discusses about the reproduction in the animal kingdom in the following verse:

> "Allah fashioned the two of a pair, the male and the female from a small quantity of liquid when it is poured out." (53:45-46)

This verse clearly mentions that all things are created in pairs and each sex performs its proper function and yet its wonderful working is part of the creative process of God.

The Quran in one verse also gives reference to the existence of animal communities:

> "There is no animal on earth, no bird which flies on wings that does not belong to communities like you. We have not neglected anything in the book of decrees. Then to their Lord they will be gathered." (6:38)

Some verses of *The Quran* mention statements concerning bees, spiders and birds. The bees are the subject of the longest commentary. These are:

> "Your Lord inspired the bees to choose your dwelling in the hills, in the trees and in what man built. Eat of all fruit and follow the ways of your Lord in humility. From within their bodies comes a liquor of different colours where is a remedy for men." (16:68-69)

The bee assimilates the juice of various kinds of flowers and fruits and forms within its body the honey which it stores in its cells of wax. The different kinds of food from which it makes its honey gives different colours to the honey e.g. it is dark brown, light-brown, yellow, white and so on. As a food it is sweet and wholesome and is used in medicine.

The Quran mentions spider in one of its verses which constitute its silken threads secreted by its gland and their calibre is infinitely fine. Naturalists are intrigued by the extraordinary pattern of work recorded by the animal's nervous cells which allows it to produce a geometrically perfect web. As *Allah* says in *The Quran*:

> "Those who choose masters other than God are like the spider when it takes for itself a dwelling. Verily, the flimsiest dwelling is the dwelling of the spider." (29:41)

This verse says that the spider's house is one of the wonderful signs of God's creation. It is made up of fine silk threads oozing out of silk glands in the spider's body. There are many kinds of spiders and spider houses.

Regarding the source of the constituents of animal milk *The Quran* is very clear. It says:

> "Verily, in cattle there is a lesson for you. We give you to drink of what is inside their bodies, coming from a conjunction between the content of the intestine and the blood, milk pure and pleasant for those who drink it." (16:16)

Earlier, it was unknown to human mind that plants too have male and female gender distinctions. Even the plants that are unisexual have distinct elements of both male and female. As *The Quran* comments:

> "*Allah* has sent down water from the sky. With it we have produced diverse pairs of plants each separate from others." (20:53)

The end products of reproduction are fruits in the superior plants which has its preceding stage in the form of the flower which contains both male and female organs in the form of the stamens and ovules.

Once pollen has been carried to the flower they bear fruit which in turns matures and frees its seeds. All fruits therefore imply the existence of male and female organs which is mentioned in *The Quran*. As *Allah* says in *The Quran*:

> "And of everything we have created in pairs." (51:49)

It is further said:

> "Glory to *Allah* who created in pairs all things that the earth produces as well as their own kind and things of which they have no knowledge." (36:36)

The mystery of sex runs through all creation in man, in animal life, in vegetable life and possibly in other things of which we have no knowledge.

Then there are pairs of opposite forces in which forces of nature e.g. positive and negative electricity etc. are present. The atom itself consists of a positively charged nucleus or proton surrounded by negatively charged electrons. The construction of matter itself is thus referred to as pairs of opposite energies.

5) Human Reproduction:

The first step of human reproduction is discussed in *The Quran,* that the fertilization is performed by only a very small volume of liquid. It repeats this concept eleven times using the following expression:

> "God fashioned man from a small quantity of sperm." (16:4)

Another verse indicates that the small quantity in question is put in a 'firmly established lodging' which obviously means the genital organs.

Allah says:

> "Then we placed man as small quantity of sperm in a safe lodging firmly established." (23:13)

This verse indicates that the growth in the foetus stage is silent and unseen. The foetus is protected in the mother's womb like a king in a castle. It is firmly fixed and gets the protection of the mother's body on which it depends for its own growth until birth.

The second step discussed in *The Quran* is regarding the constituents of the fertilizing liquid. As *The Quran* says in the following verse:

> "Verily we created man from a small quantity of mingled liquid." (76:2)

When *The Quran* talks of a fertilizing liquid composed of different components it also informs us that man's progeny will be maintained by something which may be extracted from this liquid. As it is said in the following verse:

> "God made his progeny from the quintessence of a despised liquid."(32:8)

The Arabic word translated for the word 'quintessence' is *'Sulalah'*. It also means gentle extraction from a fluid. It signifies something which is extracted, the best part of a thing.

The third step, the implantation of the egg in the female genital organs, is discussed in this following verse:

> "We cause whom we will to rest in the womb for an appointed term." (22:5)

The implantation of the egg in the uterus is the result of the development of veritable elongation of the egg which like roots in the soil draws nourishment from the thickness of the uterus necessary to the egg's growth. These formations make the egg literally cling to the uterus. This modern time discovery of the clinging of the egg is described at five different places in *The Quran*:

> "Read in the name of your Lord who created, who created man from something which clings." (96:1-2)

The Arabic word used in *The Quran* for 'which clings' is *'alaq'*, which also means a 'congealed clot of blood' and a 'leech like substance'. This verse of *The Quran* is in exact conformity with the development of modern science which was confirmed by Prof. Keith Moore, who was the Professor of Embryology and Chairman of the Department of Anatomy at the University of Toronto (Canada). Presently, he is considered one of the highest authorities in the field of Embryology.

This concept is repeated in *The Quran* in the four other following verses:

(a) "We have fashioned you from .... something which clings." (22:5)

(b) "We have fashioned the small quantity of sperm into something which clings." (23:14)

(c) "God created you from a small quantity of sperm from something which clings." (40:67)

(d) "Was (man) not a small quantity of sperm which has been poured out? After that he was something which clings; then God fashioned him in due proportion." (75:37-38)

The last step, regarding the human reproduction is the evolution of the embryo inside the uterus. After 'the thing which clings', *The Quran* informs us that the embryo passes through the stage of 'chewed flesh'. As *The Quran* mentions it:

> "We created the thing which clings into a chewed lump of flesh and we created the chewed flesh into bones and we clothed the bows with intact flesh." (23:14)

In human embryology, the first sense to develop is hearing. The foetus can hear sounds after the twenty-fourth week. The sense of sight is developed by the twenty eighth week when the retina becomes sensitive to light. *The Quran* is explicit on this point:

> "And He gave you the faculties of hearing and sight and feeling and understanding." (32:9)

It is further said:

> "Verily we have created man from a drop of mingled sperm in order to try him. So, we gave him the gift of hearing and sight." (76:2)

In all these verses the sense of hearing is mentioned before that of sight. Thus, the Quranic description matches with the discoveries in modern embryology.

The Quran has not ignored the practical aspect of human life. There are many details in *The Quran* on practical side of life including the sex life of man. As it says:

> "Man was created from a liquid poured out. It issued as a result of the conjunction of the sexual area of the man and the sexual area of the woman." (86:6-7)

The behavior of a man in his intimate relationship with his wife is explicitly stated. God gives the following command to the Prophet and says:

> "They (the believers) question the concerning menstruation. Say: This is an evil. Keep away from women during menstruation and do not approach them until they are clean. When they have purified themselves go to them as God ordered it to you." (2:222)

In the month of Ramadan, sexual relations are permitted at night. As it is mentioned in *The Quran*:

> "Permitted to you, on the night of the fast, is to break chastity with your wives. They are a garment for you and you are a garment for them. So hold intercourse with them and seek what God has ordained for you." (2:187)

This verse means that men and women are each other's garment i.e. they are for mutual support, mutual comfort and mutual protection, fitting into each other as a garment fits the body. A garment is both for show and concealment. The question of sex is always delicate to handle and a clear, open and honest course is better than fraud and self-deception.

6) General Sciences:

The Quran talks about fingerprinting method in detail 1400 years ago. In the following verses *The Quran* talks about this method:

> "Does man think that we cannot assemble his bones? Nay, we are able to put together in perfect order the very tips of his fingers." (75:3-4)

When the unbelievers argue regarding the day of judgment of the bones of dead people have disintegrated in the earth then how each individual would be identified on the day of resurrection. Almighty *Allah* answers this question in the above mentioned verse that He can not only assemble our bones but can also reconstruct perfectly our very fingertips.

This fact is further authenticated by the research of Sir Francis Golt in 1880. By this it is admitted that no two persons in the world can ever have exactly the same fingerprint pattern and this fingerprint method is accepted by the police world wide.

Another important aspect is the presence of pain receptors in the skin. Earlier it was thought that the sense of feeling and pain was only dependent on the brain. Recent discoveries proved that the pain receptors are also present in the skin without which a person would not be able to feel pain. Regarding this fact *The Quran* gives an indication:

> "Those who reject our signs, we shall soon cast into the fire as often as their skins are roasted then we shall change them for fresh skins that they taste the penalty: for *Allah* is exalted in power, wise." (4:56)

In this chapter, I have presented a brief idea of *The Quran* and Modern Science based on some current researches. I have presented only few signs presented in *The Quran* which talks about science. *The Quran* is a book of 'signs' and not a book of science. These signs invite man to realize the purpose of his existence on the earth and to maintain the harmony with nature. I pray that this humble effort is accepted by *Allah,* to whom I pray for mercy and guidance *(Aameen)*.

* * *